# TREATING THE MENTALLY ILL

Other books in the At Issue series:

# TREATING THE MENTALLY ILL

Kyla Stinnett, *Book Editor*

Bruce Glassman, *Vice President*
Bonnie Szumski, *Publisher*
Helen Cothran, *Managing Editor*

San Diego • Detroit • New York • San Francisco • Cleveland
New Haven, Conn. • Waterville, Maine • London • Munich

*For more information, contact*
Greenhaven Press
27500 Drake Rd.
Farmington Hills, MI 48331-3535
Or you can visit our Internet site at http://www.gale.com

| LIBRARY OF CONGRESS CATALOGING-IN-PUBLICATION DATA |
|---|
| Treating the mentally ill / Kyla Stinnett, book editor.<br>   p. cm. — (At issue)<br>  Includes bibliographical references and index.<br>  ISBN 0-7377-2432-3 (lib. : alk. paper) — ISBN 0-7377-2433-1 (pbk. : alk. paper)<br>   1. Mental illness—Patients—Rehabilitation. 2. Mentally ill—Treatment.<br>  I. Stinnett, Kyla. II. At issue (San Diego, Calif.)<br>  RC480.53.T746  2004<br>  616.89'1—dc22                                           2003067644 |

Printed in the United States of America

# Contents

# Introduction

One of the earliest treatments for mental illness was developed in Neolithic times, more than five thousand years ago. In a process known as trepanning, Stone Age surgeons would use a small tool to bore a hole in the skull of their patients in order to release the evil spirits believed to cause mental illness. Since that time, people have developed hundreds of treatments that today seem cruel or bizarre. For example, in 1276, Pope John XXI, the author of several medical treatises, suggested that eating a roasted mouse could cure anxiety. In the seventeenth century, French and British doctors experimented with transfusing the blood of sheep into their patients, thinking the blood of a docile creature "might tame their mad passions." In 1667 an "insane" Englishman named Arthur Coga received a transfusion of twelve ounces of sheep blood, but the treatment did not help greatly. Well-known diarist Samuel Pepys wrote that Coga was still "a little cracked in the head" despite the transfusion. After a French patient died from the treatment the following year, the practice was abandoned.

In the early nineteenth century, Benjamin Rush, a pioneer of American psychiatry, advocated some treatments that seem primitive in retrospect. One of his ideas to cure mental patients was to strap them into a gyration device that would spin them in circles for hours. Rush believed that the spinning would lower the blood pressure to the brain, calming the patients, and also "shake out" their madness. In the 1940s, psychiatrist Walter Freeman developed the transorbital lobotomy, in which an ice pick–like instrument was used to remove the frontal lobes of the brain—a treatment he claimed cured mental illnesses including schizophrenia, depression, and obsessive-compulsive disorder. In fact, of the 86 percent of patients who survived the treatment, most suffered the loss of their personalities and the ability to feel and express emotions. These losses may have made the patients' mental illnesses less of a concern to others but obviously did nothing to help the patients themselves, who often had to be retaught to eat and use the bathroom. The lobotomy operation became increasingly controversial in the 1950s and 1960s, and with the passage of laws to protect patients, is no longer legal in the United States.

## A scientific mystery

Although the treatments described above are wildly different, they share a common factor: In each case, people were trying to alleviate the symptoms of various mental disorders without knowing their cause. Scientists today have better tools to study the brain and mind, but they still do not know exactly what causes mental illness. As a result, treatment is still focused on alleviating symptoms, with varying degrees of success. Nonetheless, researchers are intensely interested in the important question of what causes mental disorders, and the debate over various theories has often been heated, if not acrimonious. Looking briefly at the history of this debate over the past century reveals how the prevailing notions of the causes of mental disorders have changed and how these beliefs have determined the kinds of treatment people receive.

In the late nineteenth century the idea that mental disorders might be caused by physical abnormalities in the brain was not new. The Greek physician Galen (130–200 B.C.) had believed that mental illnesses were the result of physical disturbances in the brain and had recommended a treatment plan including exercise and the use of herbs such as the purgative hellebore. In 1852 German physician Heinrich Laehr speculated that "an extremely small chemical and physical change in the brain . . . will suffice to produce a mental disorder." Although medical science had advanced since the era when roasted mice were a recommended treatment, in the late 1800s researchers still knew little about brain chemistry and were using their limited technical skills and tools to try to understand the functioning of the brain and its effect on mental health. However, one medical neurologist began to develop the theory that mental disorders had psychological causes rather than physical ones.

## A psychological explanation of mental disorders

Sigmund Freud was an Austrian who had become an internationally recognized expert on the causes of children's paralysis. His work with patients suffering from "hysteria" (a nineteenth-century diagnosis for symptoms including anxiety, neurosis, and mania) led him to the idea that mental illnesses are caused by unconscious desires and conflicts that form in infancy. He believed that most of these conflicts developed from a person's failure to successfully move through what he defined as the childhood stages of sexual development. Freud pioneered the psychoanalytic method in which patients talk spontaneously about their feelings under an analyst's guidance in order to discover and resolve their unconscious conflicts.

Although Freud's sexual theory and insistence that the libido is the dominant human drive is still controversial today, his concept of the unconscious and psychoanalysis has influenced millions of lives and Western culture itself. Freudian concepts and language have shaped many fields of study, including education, medicine, law, sociology, and literature. In addition, the idea that mental disorders are rooted in childhood experiences rather than purely in brain abnormalities had a profound impact on the treatment of mental illness for several decades. As psychiatrist Elliot Valenstein writes, "Although orthodox psychoanalytic therapy was practiced by only a small percentage of mental health professionals, psychoanalytic explanations of the causes of different mental disorders and the best way to treat them dominated the field."

## The "pharmacological revolution"

In the 1950s the accidental discovery of several drugs that alleviated some of the symptoms of mental disorders including schizophrenia, depression, and anxiety ushered in an era that many have called a "pharmacological revolution." At first psychiatrists prescribed these drugs to patients only as an adjunct to psychotherapy, but gradually they began to rely more on the drugs in their treatment plans and to spend less and less time providing psychotherapy to patients. Some began to denigrate psychotherapy as "just talk" and believed that there was no psychiatric problem that could not be chemically controlled. Many patients were happy to be able to have an "easy" treatment for disorders, swallowing pills instead of having long, drawn-out talking cures. As one psychiatrist recalls, "All of a sudden, we were being told, 'Gee, doc, you're great.'" Governments even began to empty and close down mental hospitals, believing that patients would be able to recover by taking medications on their own.

By the 1980s most psychologists and psychiatrists believed that medications should play an important role in the treatment of many mental disorders, and pharmaceutical companies were doing a strong business developing and selling many new kinds of medications for disorders. Toward the end of the decade, the corporation Eli Lilly developed one of the first of a new type of mood-altering drug that would soon dominate the market: Prozac. It was claimed to cure a long list of conditions, including depression, anxiety, compulsions, and eating disorders, and became hugely prescribed. Prozac sales amounted to $1.2 billion in 1993, its first year on the market. The media greatly contributed to the popularity of Prozac, producing thousands of pieces about the "miracle pill." In March 1990 *Newsweek* ran a cover story on Prozac, describing it as a medical breakthrough. *New York* magazine called it a "wonder drug." Similar mood-altering drugs, such as Zoloft, Paxil, and Luvox, were soon developed and marketed by companies that wanted a share in the profitable market Eli Lilly was enjoying.

The popularity and media coverage of these drugs has bolstered the view that mental disorders are caused by chemical imbalances. For example, the popular explanation for why drugs such as Prozac sometimes help people with mental illness is that they raise the levels of serotonin— a neurotransmitter chemical that carries signals from one nerve cell to another—in the brain. Researchers theorize that people suffering from problems such as depression and anxiety have deficient levels of the neurotransmitter. However, scientists have not yet discovered conclusive evidence that mental illness is caused by chemical imbalances. In fact, they have not even been able to measure biochemical imbalances. There are no blood tests or brain scans that can diagnose depression and other disorders. As psychiatrist Nancy Andreasen writes, "We do not really know if a biochemical imbalance is the cause of any mental disorder, and we do not know how even the hypothesized biochemical imbalances could produce the emotional, cognitive, and behavioral symptoms that characterize any mental disorder."

Despite the lack of conclusive evidence, the theory of biochemical imbalance is the predominant explanation for mental disorders today. Neuroscientist Elliot Valenstein offers a couple of reasons for the popularity of this explanation, writing that "the theories are held onto not only because there is nothing else to take their place, but also because they are useful in promoting drug treatment." Although many advances have been achieved in the areas of brain chemistry and neuropharmacology, he argues, scientists' understanding of the causes of mental illness and how drug treatments work is still "primitive."

## The future of mental health treatment

Scientists have found more advanced ways of treating mental illness than sheep-blood transfusions, gyration machines, and lobotomies, but are still at the level of developing treatments for symptoms rather than understanding the causes of mental disorders. In the past few decades, however, a great deal has been learned about the brain and the mind, and some researchers believe that the study of genetics will be a key in creating more effective treatments and possibly gaining understanding of the causes of mental illness. For example, a team at the University of Pittsburgh School of Medicine used gene-chip technology to discover a DNA mutation shared by ten schizophrenic patients in their study. The flaw was on a gene that controlled the duration of signals in a nerve cell and affected the brain's visual, motor, and cognitive centers. Team leader Pat Levitt suggests that this mutation might help explain the hallucinations and attention problems people with schizophrenia suffer. It is possible that if researchers can find individual genetic flaws, they may be able to develop tailored treatments that take into account the age, sex, and race of patients suffering from a particular condition.

Although neuroscience has played a major role in the recent developments in the treatment of mental health, the search for effective treatments will not be reduced to manipulating brain chemistry to the neglect of factors such as a person's family history, relationships, job pressures, and cultural background. The psychological component emphasized by Freud and many others is an important part of understanding and treating mental illness. As Andreasen writes, "Mental illnesses, although they have a physical component, are nonetheless also mental. Almost by definition, they are illnesses that affect the mind, however much they arise from the brain. . . . If seen only as brain diseases, [patients] are at serious risk for being dehumanized." She warns against the trend of assigning a diagnosis to patients and then treating them as though they were generic cases—a trend that has become prevalent with the ease of writing a quick prescription for an antidepressant or other drug for a particular problem. She notes that "bodies can be treated fairly generically, but minds are individual and unique." An evaluation of a person's symptoms therefore must be individualized and take into account the personal aspects of their lives that affect their minds. Furthermore, researchers seeking to understand the causes of mental illness and develop treatments will have to address both the role of the mind and the role of the brain.

Although the causes of mental disorders remain a mystery in the twenty-first century, various kinds of treatment have helped some people overcome the debilitating symptoms of mental illness. In *At Issue: Treating Mental Illness*, the authors debate the effectiveness and risks of these treatments.

# 1

# Antidepressants Help Millions of People

### Sally Satel

*Sally Satel, a practicing psychiatrist, is a lecturer at Yale University School of Medicine. She is also the W.H. Brady Fellow at the American Enterprise Institute, a conservative public policy research organization.*

The benefits of Prozac and other antidepressants far outweigh the risks of some of their side effects. Although some people have claimed that these medications have caused people to kill themselves or others, such serious side effects are extremely rare. A few people do develop suicidal tendencies after taking antidepressants due to a side effect called *akathisia*, a profound restlessness that can be so distressing that it can drive a patient to suicide. However, only a tiny percentage of patients on antidepressants develop this condition. In addition, the agitation develops relatively slowly, over the course of days or weeks. Therefore, an attentive psychiatrist should be able to observe any suicidal tendencies and hospitalize a patient if the situation becomes serious. On the positive side, antidepressants have helped countless people overcome debilitating depression and enjoy their lives again. They are thus willing to tolerate the more common side effects of antidepressants, such as insomnia, nausea, decreased appetite, and impaired sexual functioning, in order to improve their mood.

In 1988 the anti-depressant Prozac arrived and made a huge impact on both the pharmaceutical market and the culture. We have heard virtually everything about the drug: that it makes some people "better-than-well," and that it is to blame for the murders committed by one of the Columbine killers [Eric Harris, one of the students who went on a shooting rampage that killed thirteen students at Columbine High School in 1999, was taking the antidepressant Luvox]. Of course the truth lies somewhere in between, but considerably closer to the benign end of the spectrum.

Are Prozac and its relatives, Paxil, Zoloft, Effexor, and Luvox, free of side effects? Of course not. But lawsuits have been charging that these medications have caused people to kill themselves, to kill others, and even to rob banks.

As a psychiatrist, I have prescribed these anti-depressants to hundreds of people. Formally, they are classified as SRIs (serotonin reuptake inhibitors) and, yes, there can be serious side effects, but those are very rare.

---

*When there is needless alarm, of course, patients suffer.*

---

Over the years, a number of anti-Prozac books have appeared. In spring 2000, *Prozac Backlash* written by a psychiatrist, Joseph Glenmullen, was published and renewed the controversy over SRIs' safety. The claims made in that book fostered needless alarm. When there is needless alarm, of course, patients suffer. The book's claims of induced suicide, homicide, and crippling neurological disorders are vastly oversold. If I were a patient taking Prozac, I would flush my pills down the toilet after reading Glenmullen's book. I do agree that Prozac has been embraced perhaps too enthusiastically as a panacea for the human condition, but it has also extended the treatment of depression in positive ways. No longer are anti-depressants reserved for the most profoundly depressed.

## The newest anti-depressants have fewer side effects

Why have Prozac and similar drugs been used more liberally than their predecessors? First, they have fewer side effects. Blurry vision, low blood pressure, and sedation were common problems with earlier anti-depressants like the tricyclics and monamine oxidase inhibitors. In the case of monamine oxidase inhibitors, patients had to adhere to a special diet to avoid risk of stroke. Also, they are much less dangerous in overdose, something one worries about with people who may be suicidal.

Many depressed people who probably couldn't tolerate the side effects of those earlier anti-depressants have benefited. I do suspect, however, that the threshold has been lowered too far in some cases—such that individuals who didn't need anti-depressants, whose mood would have resolved on its own, or who would have responded well to psychotherapy alone—were put on medication. Most people who ask for SRIs are depressed. But Peter Kramer's book, *Listening to Prozac*, talks about the phenomenon of "cosmetic psychopharmacology" in which personality traits like shyness, perfectionism, lack of confidence, fear of intimacy, over- or under-competitiveness, even jealousy are "cured" by Prozac. Psychiatrists' prescribing of Prozac for these purposes has, not surprisingly, come under scrutiny by the profession and the pundits alike, but the most dramatic controversy has been spurred by allegations of the violent urges that Prozac and other SRIs may produce—suicide as well as assault and murder.

## The risk of suicide is low

There have been cases of people who kill themselves on Prozac. This is tragic, but it is far from a shock. After all, who are the recipients of these drugs? The risk of suicide in the general population is 1%; in the depressed population it is 15%.

One of the very first things that medical students learn is that patients are at a higher risk for suicide right after anti-depressants of any kind are initiated. Why? Because the various symptoms of depression don't resolve all at once and frequently what's first to improve are the energy level and sleep. And if a patient's energy returns but he is still utterly depressed he can mobilize himself sufficiently to attempt and complete suicide. Also, it is not unusual for patients to look a lot brighter once they have made the decision that they are going to kill themselves. They have a paradoxical mood lift, because they feel they have resolved their problem. Psychiatrists are trained to watch for this.

There have been some reports of people committing suicide on anti-depressants who hadn't previously entertained suicidal thoughts. One of the most compelling theories behind this is a side effect called akathisia, which is a profound kind of restlessness. Patients will describe feeling like their organs are writhing in their body and they just have to move. Akathisia can be so distressing as to drive a patient to suicide.

No one had reason to believe that the Prozac-type drugs would cause this side effect. It was heretofore associated with anti-psychotic drugs. But within the last decade some patients on anti-depressants did develop akathisia.

This is so rare: At least three million people a year take these medications. Over a 10-year period one study found 92 case reports of these side effects. It's a tiny percentage. But, of course, when it happens it's spectacular.

The very important point is that these phenomena don't start overnight. The intense agitation develops over a course of days or weeks. And that is why it is so important for the psychiatrist to follow the patients carefully.

That is the key: These medications are not so risky that they shouldn't be prescribed, but they should be prescribed by people who are knowledgeable and have the capacity to hospitalize a patient if the situation turns dire.

Finally, you're probably familiar with the more common side effects of SRIs: insomnia, nausea, decreased appetite, and impaired sexual functioning. These are often trade-offs that patients are willing to endure until their mood improves. And it is a good trade-off for them.

These medications help millions and millions of people. Are there some side effects? Yes. But the more dramatic incidents are enormously rare, and it is clear from the literature, and from my experience in the clinical world, that the benefits far outweigh the risks.

# 2

# Antidepressants May Cause Suicide and Violent Behavior in Children and Teenagers

## Rob Waters

*Rob Waters is a freelance journalist whose articles have appeared in* Health, Parenting, *and the* Los Angeles Times. *He is the coauthor of* From Boys to Men: A Woman's Guide to the Health of Husbands, Partners, Sons, Fathers, and Brothers.

Antidepressants including Paxil, Prozac, Zoloft, and Effexor have provoked hostile behavior and thoughts about suicide in a number of children and teenagers who have been prescribed the drugs. Some of these patients have killed themselves. Although pediatricians and child psychiatrists have been prescribing antidepressants for years, parents have usually been given no warning of the dangerous possible side effects the drugs can have on their children. However, in 2003 wide media coverage of the possible risks of Paxil for young patients contributed to a growing public awareness of the controversy over prescribing antidepressants to children. That summer the Federal Drug Administration (FDA) issued a warning that Paxil could cause children to consider or attempt suicide. The FDA is now conducting a review of pediatric clinical trials of Paxil and seven other antidepressants. The controversy has been heightened by accusations that several drug manufacturers have manipulated the data in various studies to reduce the apparent risk of antidepressants triggering violence and thoughts of suicide in young patients.

For 16-year-old Angela Reich,[1] 2002 was a year of hell. First, the Palo Alto teenager was diagnosed with a rare form of highly aggressive can-

---

1. Names and identifying details have been changed.

cer. Then she went through months of debilitating chemotherapy that made her nauseous, caused her hair to fall out and kept her in bed for much of her last year of high school. She handled it all with unflappable poise and good humor until it seemed she was out of the woods. But the worst began when she started taking the antidepressant Paxil.

"Angela had been just pushing through and pushing through," says her mother, Sara. "She mustered all her strength and courage to face the chemo and to be sick all the time." By the end of the summer, with the most intense part of her treatment behind her, she was worn out and discouraged. "She started to feel overwhelmed and depressed." She began seeing a therapist and talked openly about her feelings. But after a few weeks her depression had not lifted, and Angela asked about going on antidepressants. It took six weeks for the Reich's insurance company to approve a psychiatrist, and by then Angela was in a deep funk. "She was not wanting to get out of bed in the morning," Reich recalls. "She couldn't do her homework. She said it felt terrible to live like this, but then she would say, 'I don't want to die, I don't want to hurt myself.' I remember sitting across from her at the kitchen table and tears pouring from her eyes and her saying 'This is so hard.'"

The psychiatrist prescribed Paxil, a selective serotonin reuptake inhibitor (SSRI) similar to its famous predecessor, Prozac. On a dose of 5, then 10, then 15 milligrams a day, Angela soon started feeling better. Five weeks after she began taking the medication, Angela and her mother met with the psychiatrist, who suggested another boost in dosage. "He said she's doing well now; she could be doing even better on 20 milligrams," Reich remembers. She was hesitant, but Angela wanted her old life back and thought it made sense to try. The next day, she started on the higher dose.

## Restless legs and sleepless nights

Within days, Reich says, her daughter was acting strangely. The first change was Angela couldn't keep her leg still. "She'd be sitting in a chair and her knee would be jerking up and down." She became irritable and had more trouble sleeping. Her parents would ask about her restless, jerking leg and she would snap at them to leave her alone.

When Reich left on a business trip, Angela called her three or four times a day and begged her to come home early. When she returned, Angela "burst in my room and hugged me," Reich says. "She kept saying, 'Mommy, I'm so glad you're home.' She was scared, like she couldn't cope. She said she dreaded going to bed because she had so much trouble sleeping. She'd lay there thinking and her thoughts got darker and became unbearable."

That night, Reich shared her daughter's bed but Angela slept little and was still wound up in the morning. When her mother tried to get her ready for a piano lesson, she said she wasn't going. "She looked funny and had a weird smile on her face," Reich remembers. "I knew something was wrong. I looked around the room and saw some pill bottles. I asked if she took any pills and she said 'Yes.'"

Under questioning, Angela told her mother she had taken four tablets of the sleeping pill Ativan. Then Angela ran to the bathroom, locked the door, and started going through pill bottles. Her father, Jim, smashed the door open and snatched a bottle of Benadryl from her hands. She ran to her purse, seized a bottle of Tylenol and began shoving pills in her mouth. Her mother grabbed her, pinned her arms, and marched her to the car, as Angela's younger brother watched.

Reich drove straight to a nearby hospital. One block from the house, Angela turned to her mother. "She said 'Mom, I don't know why I did that. It was like something took me over.' And I said 'I know, it wasn't like you. But I will keep you safe.'"

At the emergency room, the staff administered charcoal to absorb the drugs, then transferred Angela to a psychiatric hospital. The next day, the hospital psychiatrist called Reich. "He told me it was a drug-induced suicide attempt," she said, related to the increased dosage of Paxil.

Neither Angela, Sara nor her husband, Jim, an internal medicine doctor, knew Paxil might carry a risk of triggering suicidal thoughts or actions. Aside from a generic statement that depressed people are more likely to attempt suicide, there is no mention of such a risk in Paxil's prescribing information.

## England acts, United States follows

The risk Paxil may pose to children and teenagers burst into the news [in the summer of 2003], when British regulators issued a warning urging doctors not to prescribe the drug to children. They were acting on new data presented to United States and British authorities showing that among 1,100 children enrolled in clinical trials of Paxil, those taking the drug were nearly three times as likely to consider or attempt suicide as children taking placebos. "There is an increase in the rate of self-harm and potentially suicidal behavior in this age group," said a statement from the British Medicines and Healthcare Products Regulatory Agency (MHRA). "It has become clear that the benefits (of Paxil) in children for the treatment of depressive illness do not outweigh these risks."

Nine days later, the FDA [Federal Drug Administration] issued a similar warning and announced that it would conduct a detailed review of pediatric trials of Paxil, a review soon broadened to include seven other antidepressants, including top sellers Prozac, Zoloft and Effexor. In August, Wyeth Pharmaceuticals warned doctors that its drug, Effexor, triggered hostile behavior or suicidal thinking in children at twice the rate as the sugar pills taken as placebos. Then [in December 2003], the MHRA announced that it was urging doctors to stop prescribing a group of six antidepressants, including Paxil, Zoloft and Effexor because they caused an increase in suicidal thoughts and actions. "These products should not be prescribed as new therapy for patients under 18 years of age with depressive illness," wrote Gordon Duff, chairman of the MHRA's Committee on Safety of Medicines, in a "Dear colleague" letter to British physicians.

Prozac, the only SSRI approved for use in depressed children, was not included in the new warning. The British review did not find a significant increase in the risk of suicide-related events among children taking the drug.

The British and American warnings were a stunning turnaround that left thousands of parents whose children are using the drugs wondering whether their children were at risk. But it was also long-sought vindication for a small group of researchers, family members and lawyers who have been arguing for years that antidepressants cause some people to become violently unhinged. They say they've been frustrated in getting this word out to the public, in large part because of the FDA's unwillingness to confront and control the drugmakers.

The FDA's warning about a possible suicide risk from Paxil left Sara and Jim Reich feeling furious, betrayed, and ready to sue. "Had I known there was a threefold increased risk of suicide among kids taking Paxil, I would not have allowed my daughter to go on that drug," said Jim. In fact, Jim has prescribed the drug himself and is outraged that the Physician's Desk Reference, or PDR—the drug bible for doctors, based on FDA-approved prescribing information—says nothing about Paxil's suicide risk.

The British and American warnings also raised some troubling questions: How did drugs that have been widely promoted as nearly risk-free, and that are commonly prescribed by pediatricians and child psychiatrists, come to be seen as potentially dangerous? What should parents whose children are taking them do about it? And just how effective are these drugs that can sometimes cause such serious problems?

## An uncontrolled experiment

Since 1987, when Prozac became the first SSRI on the market, America's love affair with antidepressants has worked its way down the age ladder. Between 1987 and 1996, the use of antidepressants and other psychotropic medications by children and adolescents tripled, with most of that increase occurring after 1991, according to a recent study in the *Archives of Pediatric and Adolescent Medicine*. By 1996, the study found, 6 percent of American children and teenagers were taking psychotropic medications, one-third of which were antidepressants.

Biological solutions to behavioral problems were becoming increasingly acceptable, even fashionable. "I think there's been a revolution in the way people think about behavior," says Lawrence Diller, a behavioral pediatrician in Walnut Creek [California]. "The idea that children's behavior is the product primarily of their genetics and biochemistry was promoted by American psychiatry and hijacked by the drug industry. It's simply become more acceptable to see behavior as a reflection of an imbalance in chemistry rather than an imbalance in life."

The phenomenal growth in antidepressants prescribed to children leaves many doctors and therapists uneasy. Diller, who has written about his misgivings in two books (*Running on Ritalin* and *Should I Medicate My Child?*), cautiously prescribes antidepressants to some children, but says the new data about a possible link to suicide is making both him and some parents think twice. "It hasn't caused me to stop using SSRIs, particularly in teenagers, but I think it's another reminder that our information is incomplete."

To understand how we got here, it's important to know a bit about the drug-approval process. When a drug company applies to the FDA for approval to sell a medication, it must demonstrate that the drug is safe and effective for a particular population, such as adults, and a specific condition, such as depression. Once the drug has been cleared by the FDA and is on the market, doctors are free to prescribe it to anyone for any reason.

"Off-label" prescribing, is quite common; the only real restriction is that drug companies cannot market drugs to unapproved groups. From 1987, when Prozac was first approved for adults, until early [2003], when Prozac became the first SSRI approved for use in depressed children 7 and older, all antidepressants used by depressed children were prescribed off-label.

---

*The widespread use of antidepressants by children, critics say, amounts to an uncontrolled national experiment.*

---

The widespread use of antidepressants by children, critics say, amounts to an uncontrolled national experiment. The prescribing physicians are often pediatricians or family doctors with little or no training in psychopharmacology. The drugs are frequently given in the absence of therapy or other interventions. The subjects of the experiment—children—are too young to give meaningful consent. There is little understanding of the long-term effect these medications have on the architecture of children's developing brains. And the evidence that the drugs are effective is less than impressive.

When Prozac was approved for depressed children [in 2003], it was on the strength of two controlled trials. One, published in 1997 in the *Archives of General Psychiatry*, found that after eight weeks, 56 percent of kids taking Prozac showed some improvement, according to the clinicians who evaluated them, compared with 33 percent of the kids in the placebo group. But 69 percent of the kids taking Prozac still had significant symptoms of depression. Clinical trials of Paxil, Zoloft and Effexor found those drugs to be no more effective than placebos in treating depressed children.

Perhaps the most notable finding from clinical trials of antidepressants is how many children respond well to placebos—as many as 59 percent in some studies. This high placebo response rate is a common finding in pediatric drug trials, in which children are generally seen once or twice a week by clinicians, says David Healy, an internationally known psychopharmacologist from the University of Wales College of Medicine who has emerged as a prominent critic of drug company practices. "This suggests that simple support can help children in many cases," Healy says.

## SSRIs: cleaner and safer?

In the years since 1987, SSRIs have developed a reputation for being largely free of serious side effects, vastly improved over the older generation of so-called tricyclic antidepressants. In some respects, this is true: Distressed patients who attempt to kill themselves by overdosing are unlikely to succeed; they can usually tolerate the pills. And patients taking tricyclics are more likely to suffer from constipation, urinary retention, blurred vision and dry mouth.

But SSRIs cause sexual problems at fairly high rates, as well as insominia, nausea, dizziness and other side effects. Studies also have not found them to be more effective than the older pills at relieving symptoms of depression. "The SSRIs have sold themselves very heavily as safe and clean drugs compared to the old antidepressants," says Healy. "Well, it's not clear that they're safer, and it's not clear that they cause fewer side effects."

One side effect of SSRIs, recognized for at least 15 years, is a sensation called akathisia, a restless agitation that ranges from jitteriness to a sensation described by some people as "jumping out of their skin." Healy believes akathisia is the principal trigger for impulsive violence in some people taking SSRIs. "They became anxious, agitated, terrified, unable to sleep at night and restless," he says—the symptoms that plagued Angela Reich.

There have long been signs that SSRIs sometimes cause these reactions, which drug manufacturers have tried mightily, and largely successfully, to keep out of the public eye and off the labels. This issue first arose a couple years after Prozac went on the market, amid a raft of media reports about grisly acts of murder and suicide. The most notorious event took place in 1989, when Joseph Wesbecker went on a shooting frenzy, killing nine fellow workers of a Louisville, Kentucky, printing plant before turning his gun on himself. Wesbecker, who had a history of mental problems, was taking Prozac. No one could prove Prozac caused his rampage, but by early 1991, some 350 suicides of Prozac patients had been reported to the FDA, according to one former FDA official. Those reports, which occurred outside the context of scientific clinical trials, were dismissed as anecdotal and sensational by company officials.

Harder to dismiss, though, was a study published by Harvard researcher Martin Teicher and two colleagues in the *American Journal of Psychiatry* in 1990 about six patients who developed "violent suicidal preoccupation" after taking Prozac for two to seven weeks. "It was also remarkable how violent these thoughts were," the authors reported. "Two patients fantasized, for the first time, about killing themselves with a gun," they wrote, while one placed a loaded gun to her head, another had to be restrained to prevent self-mutilation, and another fantasized about killing himself in a gas explosion. None of the patients was suicidal when they started taking Prozac, the researchers reported, and their fixation with violence and death abated when they stopped.

---

*Clinical trials of Paxil, Zoloft and Effexor found those drugs to be no more effective than placebos in treating depressed children.*

---

Similar symptoms were noted the next year in a paper in the *American Journal of Child and Adolescent Psychiatry* about six children ages 10 to 17 who developed "intense self-injurious ideation or behavior" while taking Prozac. After three weeks on the drug, one 14-year-old girl, who had been depressed but never suicidal, began cutting and otherwise injuring herself. She told hospital staff, "I'm just waiting for the opportunity to kill myself," and chanted, "Kill, kill, kill; die, die, die; pain, pain, pain," according to the paper. The Yale University authors noted the complexity of reaching any conclusion about the cause of these events since the children all had lengthy histories of psychiatric difficulties that put them at risk for suicide. They also noted that many children taking Prozac become agitated, restless, and disinhibited and developed insomnia to boot.

A 1998 paper by Roger Lane, a scientist at Pfizer, the maker of Zoloft, stated that "all SSRIs have the rare potential to cause akathisia." In its most extreme form, Lane wrote, patients may feel that "death is a welcome result."

Lane also warned that akathisia can sometimes be mistaken for worsening depression, prompting some doctors to increase the dosage—and the danger. Healy agrees. "[Doctors] have been educated to think that SSRIs take four, five, six weeks to work," he says. "But they can cause problems long before that."

In response to the Teicher paper and the growing media furor connecting Prozac to acts of violence and suicide, the FDA in September 1991 convened an extraordinary special hearing of its Psychopharmacological Drugs Advisory Committee. Speakers told of family members who committed suicide or homicide while on Prozac and begged agency officials to ban or restrict the drug. But representatives of Eli Lilly, maker of the blockbuster drug, backed by FDA and academic researchers, argued that suicide is an inherent risk among depressed patients. The Lilly officials presented figures from the company's clinical trials database suggesting that people on Prozac were at no greater risk of suicide than people taking placebos.

Committee members voted unanimously in Lilly's favor, and Prozac remained on the market. No warning that the drug might induce violent or suicidal urges in some people was added to its label.

## "Cooking the books"

The Prozac suicide controversy, and the huge number of suicide reports that were streaming into the agency, reverberated inside the FDA, where two other SSRIs, Paxil and Zoloft, were being considered for approval. The FDA medical officer charged with reviewing Paxil's safety and efficacy data was Martin Brecher, now an executive with the British pharmaceutical company Astra Zeneca. "The reports of successful suicide were coming in in bunches," he said in a recent deposition. "It was extraordinary, especially in comparison to other annual reports where, you know, you had 20 reports of a cold and maybe two reports of some liver enzyme elevations and here you are with 20 deaths in a report."

Because Paxil and Zoloft were members of the same chemical class as Prozac, the FDA asked officials at SmithKline Beecham (the predecessor to GlaxoSmithKline) and Pfizer, Zoloft's maker, to submit reviews on the drugs' effect on suicidal behavior of patients. Brecher called Thomas Donnelly, a SmithKline Beecham executive, and asked him to prepare such a report. In an internal company memo uncovered in a lawsuit, Donnelly described his conversation with Brecher, noting that the FDA "does not see it as a real issue but rather as a public relations problem."

What happened next is controversial. Critics charge that the company manipulated data to diminish the apparent suicide risk among Paxil users and submitted it to the agency. One of the harshest critics is an unlikely plaintiff's attorney in San Rafael [California], a self-described conservative Republican and retired Navy officer named Don Farber.

Farber, who has spent the better part of the past five years suing GlaxoSmithKline and other drug companies, is one of a handful of lawyers handling such cases. His first case involved a San Jose man, Reynaldo Lacuzong, who, in 1996, drowned his two children and himself in a bathtub three days after he began taking Paxil. After the suit was filed, GlaxoSmithKline and the surviving Lacuzong family resolved the case with an undisclosed settlement.

The same thing has happened in dozens of other cases of alleged SSRI-induced suicide or violence; few cases ever go to jury. In June 2001, however, a case did. Three years earlier, Donald Schell, a 60-year-old Wyoming man, killed his wife, daughter and granddaughter three hours after taking two tablets of Paxil given to him as samples by his internist. Surviving family members sued GlaxoSmithKline, and the jury awarded them $6.4 million for the wrongful deaths of their relatives.

"[The company] knew there was a small group at risk and Don Schell was one of those vulnerable people," the family's attorney, Andy Vickery told the jury. Farber makes the same argument: Drug companies have an obligation to warn doctors and patients that these drugs can pose a threat to some people. "If there was a warning that said 'Caution: this drug may cause suicide in some people,' then doctors are going to know about it," Farber says.

---

*By early 1991, some 350 suicides of Prozac patients had been reported to the FDA.*

---

Instead of warning people, Farber charges, GlaxoSmithKline [GSK] tried to hide the true numbers. "They cooked the books," says Farber during a recent interview. "They cheated on the results. And the FDA is part of this."

Farber says the company manipulated the figures. Documents obtained by *The San Francisco Chronicle* show that in its initial application to the FDA, the company reported that out of 2,963 adults taking Paxil during clinical trials in the United States or other countries, seven patients killed themselves and 42 attempted suicide. But in a review submitted in April 1991, in response to Brecher's request, the seven suicides had dropped to five and the 42 attempts had gone down to 40.

At the same time, the number of attempted suicides by patients taking placebos doubled from three to six in the later review. The 1991 review also acknowledges that two suicides and two suicide attempts charged to placebo occurred during a one-week "washout" period that came before the start of the study. During that period, subjects were taken off any drugs they had been using to get the drugs out of their system. Experts say it is inappropriate to count events during the run-in period as placebo events.

Company officials admit there were errors made in reports filed with the FDA, but deny any attempt to mislead. "There were unfortunately some inconsistencies in how the data on suicide attempts was presented to FDA," says GSK spokeswoman Mary Anne Rhyne. "When we became aware of this, we went back and looked at the clinical trial data again. GSK did not intentionally submit any erroneous or misleading information to FDA. The suicide data submitted to FDA explicitly identified when events occurred during the placebo run-in period. FDA had all this information right from the beginning." Farber contends that these small shifts in numbers make a big difference in suicide rates. He claims that a close look at the data reveals that only one placebo patient out of 554 attempted suicide, while 49 patients out of 2,963 taking the drug committed or attempted suicide—a ninefold difference.

Rhyne disputes this analysis. "The randomized, placebo-controlled data shows no statistically significant differences in suicides or suicide attempts between Paxil and placebo," she says.

## Drug firms and the FDA: too close?

For its review of all pediatric trials of antidepressants, the FDA is reanalyzing the data to determine whether reports of suicidal ideation among children were categorized properly. Critics are concerned that this reanalysis may minimize the apparent suicide risk to the benefit of drug companies, and contend that the agency has a long history of protecting the industry. They point to company memos, uncovered through legal actions, that reveal a sense of confidence within the companies that the FDA was on their side. Memos from Eli Lilly executives described one FDA official, Paul Leber, as "our defender" and cautioned that faxes should not be sent to him unless he knew they were coming so he could receive them personally.

Other memos suggest Lilly officials went to great lengths to conceal any hints that Prozac might trigger suicide. Consider this line from a 1990 memo to Lilly executive Leigh Thompson written by Claude Bouchy, a Lilly official in Germany, in response to a request to change the description of an event from "suicidal ideation" to "depression." Bouchy writes: "Hans [a fellow Lilly employee] has medical problems with these directions and I have great concerns about it. I do not think I could explain to the BGA [the German FDA], a judge, to a reporter, or even to my family why we would do this, especially on the sensitive issue of suicide and suicidal ideation."

Critics charge that the pro-industry stance of FDA officials prevented a more thorough examination of the role antidepressants may play in triggering suicide and violence in some users. They also charge that many American psychiatric researchers have been compromised in their ability to look objectively at this issue because they are so dependent on funding from pharmaceutical companies.

The FDA's Thomas Laughren rejects the notion that his agency is protecting drugmakers. "The goal here is to get to the truth," he says. For the review of pediatric trials of antidepressants now under way, the agency is bringing in a panel of experts as judges. "We're taking all the cases and having them reclassified blindly," he says. "They'll be looking at all the information that is relative to the question of suicidality and they will not know the drug assignment."

As the agency reviews the data, experts will debate a core question: how to reconcile reports of antidepressants triggering suicidal behavior with other studies that suggest that these drugs reduce suicide rates. A paper published in the October [2003] *Archives of General Psychiatry* found that regions of the country where the use of antidepressants by children increased the most also tended to have the greatest drop in suicide rates. Could antidepressants lower the suicide risk in some people while raising it in others? "It's entirely possible that both things are true," says Mark Olfson, a professor of clinical psychiatry at Columbia University and lead author of the *Archives* paper.

David Healy says the drugs simply have different effects on different people. "My hunch is that, just as with adults, there is a group of children who are suited to the pills and do very well on them and an equally large group of kids who are not." Among those who don't do well, Healy says, are some who get much worse.

One thing most experts seem to agree on is that patients, especially children, should be monitored closely for side effects from the day they start taking the drugs. "They may be more anxious or have unusual thoughts they've never had before," Healy says. "They may think about harming others or themselves." Healy also suggests asking children if they've had strange dreams, nightmares or thoughts since they started taking the drug. "The other thing to look out for," he says, "is the opposite effect: Kids who become absolutely fearless, they just don't feel anxious at all."

## Tragedy strikes

On Feb. 2 [2004], nearly 13 years after the 1991 Prozac hearings, an FDA advisory committee will once again hold a hearing about the risk of suicide by people taking antidepressants, this time focusing on the risk to children and teenagers. The meeting will come too late to help 17-year-old Julie Woodward of North Wales, Pennsylvania.

In July [2003], Julie began attending a two-week group therapy program at nearby Horsham Clinic. A break-up with a boyfriend and conflicts with her parents had left her feeling withdrawn and in a struggle to maintain good grades. One condition of attending the program was taking antidepressants, Tom Woodward says. He and his wife didn't really like the idea, but were told they were "essential to treatment" and "very benign." On day three of the program, Julie began taking 50 milligrams of Zoloft, and that night came the first signs of unusual behavior. Julie and her mother had a small dispute, and Julie roughly shoved her mother, an out-of-character act, Woodward says.

*Critics charge that the pro-industry stance of FDA officials prevented a more thorough examination of the role antidepressants may play in triggering suicide and violence in some users.*

During the next few days, Julie became more edgy and withdrawn. On the evening of day six, she told her parents she wanted to stay home alone. But when they looked for her later that night, they couldn't find her. The next day, her father found her body hanging in the garage. One week after starting on Zoloft, she had taken her life.

When the FDA hearing comes, Tom and Kathy Woodward plan to testify, as do Jennifer Tierney and her daughter, Jame, of Kernerville, North Carolina. The Tierneys' story exemplifies another part of the anti-depressant story: withdrawal.

---

*All SSRIs have been reported to cause withdrawal problems in some patients who stop taking them.*

---

All SSRIs have been reported to cause withdrawal problems in some patients who stop taking them. Paxil and Effexor, however, seem especially likely to trigger withdrawal symptoms, probably because they exit a user's body more rapidly. "Paxil has been linked to more reports of withdrawal symptoms than any other drug in clinical history," says Karen Barth, an attorney with Baum-Hedlund, a Los Angeles firm that is representing some 3,000 people who have suffered withdrawal problems on Paxil. Jame Tierney was 14 when she was prescribed Effexor to ease migraines she'd been suffering from for years. She started with Effexor and other drugs, but gradually went off the others. She enjoyed eight good months of reduced headache pain. Then the migraines worsened and her neurologist doubled the dose. Within two weeks, her personality began to change. "She became the most angry, combative, raging child you've ever seen," says her mother. "I'd never seen her like this and I had no idea why." Jame was also unhappy and depressed. "I was hopeless, and I thought suicide was the only way out," she recalls. "I had violent thoughts and tendencies that I'd never felt before." She contemplated killing herself and made one attempt to cut her wrists.

She remained on 150 milligrams and in a raging misery for a full year, functioning at school but isolating herself in her room. Then her mother learned Effexor wasn't a headache drug but an antidepressant, unapproved for children, which can sometimes cause serious side effects. Over the objections of the neurologist, Jame tried to taper off the drug. Her personality quickly returned to normal, but she suffered terrible withdrawal symptoms—constant vomiting, headaches, muscle aches and disequilibrium that kept her out of school for months. Finally, on advice from a California doctor, she began taking vitamin and enzyme supplements. After six months, the withdrawal symptoms ended and her headaches are now a rare event. Her bout with depression, which she experienced only on Effexor, also came to an end.

While Jame was weaning herself from Effexor, Angela Reich was trying to get off Paxil. Her dose was cut to 15 milligrams a day while she got through the next round of chemo. She lowered her dosage—to 12.5 mgs, then 10, then 7.5, 5, and 2.5 over four weeks. Finally, on Jan. 24, she took no Paxil. That's when the side effects began.

"She couldn't sit up, she had trouble walking, and she was dizzy," Sara recalls. "She couldn't walk straight, and she had this zapping, this electrical feeling in her arms." The restless akathisia was gone, but Angela was uncomfortable, depressed, and irritable—"really irritable," her mother says. One night, Angela nearly flipped out. She ran into the living room, screaming, and started grabbing books off the shelves and heaving them. "She tore them up and said she hated them, she hated us and she hated the people around her," Sara says. "Then she grabbed for some knives." Her father restrained her and held her until she calmed down. But the whole family was shaken. "I started to feel like 'Oh my God, my kid has gone insane,'" Sara says.

Somehow Angela and her family got through the next month, and she gradually started to feel normal. She went off to college in September and is doing well, her parents say. Best of all, as this article was going to press, she got another negative biopsy report on her cancer.

Angela didn't want to talk about her Paxil experiences with a reporter—"It's just too painful," her mother explained. But she did want to join the lawsuit that Baum-Hedlund is pursuing against GlaxoSmithKline. "She wants to prevent anyone else from going through this kind of nightmare. She wants to save other people from suffering like she suffered."

# 3

# Physicians Are Prescribing Powerful Psychotropic Drugs for Everyday Unhappiness

Ronald W. Dworkin

*Ronald W. Dworkin is a practicing physician and an adjunct senior fellow at the Hudson Institute, a public policy organization.*

In the last thirty years, the number of patients diagnosed with depression has doubled. The sharp increase in these diagnoses is due to the fact that the medical community has blurred the distinction between everyday unhappiness and clinical depression. As a result, doctors are increasingly prescribing powerful psychotropic drugs such as Prozac to people who are suffering from the normal low spirits everyone is subject to from time to time. One reason that doctors aggressively prescribe drugs is the widely believed theory that both major mood disorders and mild unhappiness are determined by neurotransmitters in the brain. Although this theory has not been proved, it appeals to people who want to believe that happiness can be found in a pill.

The use of psychotropic medication in depressed patients has increased in the United States by more than 40 percent over the last decade, from 32 million office visits resulting in a drug prescription to over 45 million. This is in marked contrast to the period between 1978 and 1987, when the number of office visits resulting in a psychotropic drug prescription remained relatively stable. The bulk of the increase can be accounted for by the aggressive use of SSRIs (selective serotonin reuptake inhibitors) in patients. It is the class of drugs that includes Prozac, Zoloft, and Paxil. The question is: Are more Americans clinically depressed now than in the past, or has medical science started to treat the far more common experience of "everyday unhappiness" with medication, thereby increasing the number of drug prescriptions?

No one knows the answer to this question. We do know that the number of patients diagnosed with depression has doubled over the last

30 years, without any great change in diagnostic criteria. But this simply raises another question: Are doctors more aggressive in diagnosing depression, or are they simply diagnosing "everyday unhappiness" as a variant of depression and reporting it as such?

These questions are at the center of a major debate within the medical community over who the new patients being treated with antidepressants are and what treatment guidelines are being used. There is suspicion among some doctors that it is not the sickest patients who are being given psychotropic drugs but those patients who complain the loudest about being unhappy. Some physicians blame managed care for the problem of over-prescription. Because the office environment under managed care is so rushed and impersonal, many doctors take the path of least resistance by prescribing medication whenever a patient is feeling "blue." Also, managed-care companies save money when depressed patients receive medication rather than an indefinite number of counseling sessions.

This suspicion is well founded, but the origin of the problem does not lie solely in managed care. The sources of over-prescription are much more complex. Physicians are being encouraged to think about everyday unhappiness in ways that make them more likely to treat it with psychotropic medication. It is part of a growing phenomenon in our society: the medicalization of unhappiness.

In the past, medical science cared for the mentally ill, while everyday unhappiness was left to religious, spiritual, or other cultural guides. Now, medical science is moving beyond its traditional border to help people who are bored, sad, or experiencing low self-esteem—in other words, people who are suffering from nothing more than life.

---

*[Antidepressants] are merely another form of stupefaction.*

---

This trend first became widely known with the publication in 1992 of *Listening to Prozac.* Peter Kramer's book, which became a national bestseller, described the positive benefits enjoyed by depressed patients when they were put on Prozac. The drug apparently increased self-esteem and reduced negative feelings when nothing else could. The book led many in the medical community and the broader public to look more favorably on a liberal use of antidepressants.

Medical science should aggressively use drugs like Prozac for patients suffering from clinical depression. This is totally appropriate—and important. But medical science errs when it supposes that a connection exists between everyday unhappiness and clinical depression, something it increasingly does. It is hard to know where everyday unhappiness ends and clinical depression begins, and there is no easy way to distinguish between borderline depression (i.e., low spirits without any physical signs or symptoms) and everyday unhappiness. Traditionally, doctors have relied on their wisdom, intuition, and personal experience to separate the two. Such a method is neither precise nor foolproof, but it is possibly the best we can aspire to. The problem is that medical science has placed everyday unhappiness and depression on a single continuum, thereby interfering with the efforts of doctors to make fine but necessary distinctions.

Medical science has adopted a method of classifying mental disorders that blurs the line between sickness and health. And more radically, it has embraced a theory that explains all mental states in terms of their biochemical origins. Medical science has done this in order to make the problem of unhappiness simpler and more comprehensible to doctors. But the new science actually works against the efforts of doctors to separate everyday unhappiness from depression. The upshot is that physicians are more likely to treat mere unhappiness the way they would treat serious mental illness—with psychotropic drugs.

## Categories of unhappiness

One way that science establishes a link between clinical depression and everyday unhappiness is through a diagnostic instrument called the DSM. First published in 1952 and now in its fifth edition, the DSM (Diagnostic and Statistical Manual of Mental Disorders) is the essential diagnostic tool in the psychiatric field. It is a classification scheme for the entire range of human mental pathology. The DSM includes 16 major diagnostic classes (e.g., mood disorders, anxiety disorders, substance-abuse disorders), and these categories are divided up again and again in accordance with certain signs and symptoms. The DSM was originally developed by psychiatrists and psychologists, but even primary-care physicians refer to its nomenclature and categories in determining whether or not a patient has a significant mental illness.

The original purpose of the DSM was to satisfy the psychiatric profession's need for statistical and epidemiological data. But by establishing a relationship between clinical depression and everyday unhappiness when no such relationship existed before, the DSM has led inexorably to a liberal use of psychotropic medication.

Prior to the development of the DSM, feelings of unhappiness were not considered related to any of the authentic disease states that existed in medical science, such as depression or schizophrenia. While clinical depression had an official status in medical science, everyday sadness did not. The DSM changed this by creating large categories of mental illness and then ever-increasing subcategories, replete with subtypes and specifiers. "Major depression," for example, was broken down into a host of subtypes, including "minor depression," which was broken down further into symptoms of everyday unhappiness like pessimism, hopelessness, and despair. With the creation of the DSM, everyday unhappiness suddenly gained a fixed position in medical science, if only as a subcategory of a subcategory of a major mental illness. . . .

The problem arises because the categories of mental illness in the DSM are so porous as to allow everyday unhappiness to pass into the category of a more significant disease. The diagnosis of "minor depression," for example, requires only a feeling of sadness and a loss of pleasure in daily activities—a mood that may characterize the pain of everyday life as well as any medical pathology. Because "minor depression" often gets treated with medication, so too does everyday unhappiness.

"Adjustment disorder with depressed mood" is another DSM category that has the potential to be confused with everyday emotional trouble.

Included in this diagnostic group would be the person who is sad and tearful because of some painful event, like the termination of a romantic relationship or a sudden business difficulty. Distinguishing an adjustment disorder from the despondency that people might feel during one of life's routine downturns can be very difficult. Because adjustment disorders are often treated with medication, everyday unhappiness is too.

Another catch-all category is "Depressive Disorder NOS (Not Otherwise Specified)." An example of a patient with "Depressive Disorder NOS" was described to me by a psychiatrist as someone who says, "Doctor, I'm feeling sad and my sleep is restless. I don't know if I'm depressed or getting depressed, but I'm feeling down. My appetite is fine and I've got plenty of energy, but I'm unhappy." Such a patient may be a candidate for antidepressants.

---

*Depressed persons equate the pleasant mood evoked by psychoactive drugs with happiness.*

---

Doctors have long recognized this deficiency of the DSM, but it was not a serious problem in 1952 when it was created. Psychotropic medications were not as readily available as they are now, so doctors could not use drugs to treat everyday unhappiness even if they had wanted to. With the development of psychotropic medications, doctors now can. The combination of safe, effective drugs like Prozac and a relatively imprecise method of categorizing mental pathology results in a wide use of psychotropic medication in borderline cases of depression.

Many psychiatrists argue that over-prescription is largely the fault of primary-care physicians, who provide the majority of mental-health care in this country. In the view of the psychiatrists, primary-care physicians are not sufficiently well versed in the nuances of the DSM to use it properly. In one study, over 30 percent of the family practitioners interviewed confessed to needing further training to treat emotional disorders, even though it was part of their routine practice to do so. But even though mental-health professionals are more experienced in treating depression, patients do not want to be referred to a psychiatrist or therapist for fear of the stigma attached—the fear of being thought "crazy." For this reason, they insist on being treated in the primary-care setting, where expertise in managing mental illness is not great. Again, the result is an increased use of psychotropic medication in cases of everyday emotional trouble.

## A theory of moods

While the potential for diagnostic error may cause some doctors to think twice about aggressively writing drug prescriptions, a new medical theory actually justifies the liberal use of psychotropic drugs. Doctors now point to a biochemical mechanism that comes close to uniting serious mental pathology and everyday emotional trouble under a single principle. It is called the "biogenic amine theory."

According to this theory, blocking the reuptake of serotonin or other neurotransmitters in the brain has a positive effect on the human psyche.

Chemical compounds like serotonin, dopamine, noradrenalin, and acetylcholine are the means of communication across nerves. Since many of the drugs used to treat depression increase the amount of these neurotransmitters available in nerve spaces (called synapses), it is reasoned that depression might be caused by a deficiency of amines at the level of the nerve junction.

The biogenic amine theory has been in existence for several decades. It was developed through a series of inferences after the first generation of antidepressants, called tricyclics, was created. Because these drugs brought about an improvement in mood, and because they had a specific effect on the amines in nerve terminals, researchers concluded that amines must regulate mood.

While Kramer's *Listening to Prozac* examined the effects of Prozac on patients who were clinically ill, new research focuses on the effects of Prozac and other SSRIs on everyday unhappiness. According to medical science, the normal spectrum of individual differences in mood and social behavior may be tied to the same mechanism of neurotransmission that governs real mental pathology. One study postulates that different components of the human personality may have their own neurochemical substrates. These unique substrates, such as dopamine and serotonin—the same substrates involved in the biochemistry of clinical depression—may modulate the expression of everyday happiness and sadness.

Physicians have this theory in the back of their minds when they see depressed patients. They admit that depression may have many causes, but they still insist that moods are ultimately determined at the neuronal junctions of the brain where antidepressants work. In their view, all unhappiness necessarily leads back to these junctions in the same way that all roads once led to Rome.

This mindset prepares the way for a broad use of antidepressants. Because the DSM is a relatively arbitrary classification scheme, physicians think that even though their depressed patients may not fit the necessary diagnostic criteria for depression, they "almost do." . . .

## The flaw in the biogenic amine theory

The neuronal junctions of the brain where psychotropic drugs exert their effect are looked upon by medical science as a kind of corridor between matter and mood. Here at the subcellular level, the mystery of the human mood is believed to play itself out. A quantum of neurotransmitters is released at the neuronal junctions and a person's mood either rises or flags. The feeling of happiness gains an absolute unit of measurement in medical science and becomes, for all practical purposes, a visible phenomenon.

The flaw in this theory can be understood in the following way: Matter and mood are two different phenomena, as different as light and air, and so can have no physical interface. Just as light and air cannot affect one another, since there is no place in the universe where they "meet," neither can matter and mood affect one another, since there is no place in the physical world where they meet. One is finite, the other is infinite; the two are composed of different substances and so can never be joined together in physical reality.

It is true that neuronal junctions exist in the brain and that complex changes occur within these junctions during mental activity. But this does not necessarily make them a place where matter and mood share a common boundary. To say that they do is like watching a person get into a car, then seconds later watching the car move, and from this observation making the deduction that the car moves because someone gets into it. It is a false science to infer from the study of matter a knowledge any deeper than that of knowing the forms of matter and their relationships. It is a false science to say that on the basis of material knowledge, one can pretend to "know" and understand the emotional experience of life.

Kramer suggests that feelings like homesickness or loneliness are mediated through neurotransmitters like serotonin, or possibly encoded in neurons, and the fact that Prozac eases these conditions seems to confirm this view. But the notion that matter and mood can have a direct connection with one another—that somewhere at the neuronal junction, loneliness and serotonin "meet"—is tantamount to saying that the human mood is material, and that it can be touched by matter. Buried within the biogenic amine theory is an illogical belief—that neurotransmitters are shedding their physical existence, becoming even smaller than atoms, and ultimately merging with pure thought or idea. . . .

## Creating virtual realities

But what about drugs like alcohol or narcotics? They alter our moods when ingested, producing feelings like euphoria and indifference. Is this not a case of matter affecting mood by way of a common border inside the brain?

No, it is not, and this is key to understanding how drugs like antidepressants really work. Alcohol and narcotics do not produce such feelings by being received directly into the "substance" of human emotions. On the contrary, they simply alter human consciousness in a way that allows the mind to shift its mood. These drugs work by dampening certain aspects of brain function—they create an altered mental state—such that true reality becomes concealed from a person's consciousness. The dampened brain functions allow a person to imagine an alternate "reality" that is generally more pleasing.

For example, when a man contrasts his humble circumstances with some ideal of success, tension arises in his psyche. His conscience berates him, and he feels the well-known misery of failure. He might try some diversion, like golf or stamp-collecting, in order to hide from himself what he does not want to face, but sometimes the diversion does not sufficiently block the sight of things that he dislikes. So he starts to drink, and the alcohol alters his consciousness in such a way that he is diverted. After ingesting alcohol, the eye of his mind no longer sees the images that were causing him so much pain. At this point, the man starts to feel better, even "happier."

Drinking is a reliable method of dealing with unhappiness not because it exerts a direct effect on a person's mood but because it helps conceal from view what he does not want to see. It is by dampening or altering brain functions and by affecting consciousness that alcohol transforms how we feel.

It is the same with antidepressants. They are merely another form of stupefaction. True, people who take them because they are unhappy are not like alcoholics or drug addicts—they function at work, they are well mannered, and they do not vomit in the streets. But although their method is "cleaner," they are attempting the same thing as the person who uses alcohol to raise his spirits. Unlike the drunk, their minds remain awake, clear, and lucid, but the drugs have still tampered with their brain functions, hiding from them what they do not want to see.

---

*Medical science should confine itself to the treatment of clinical depression.*

---

This point was revealed to me in the case of one friend who was taking Prozac for general unhappiness, though not under my supervision. He said, "I feel a lot better. I don't have to look into the abyss anymore. I see my problems, but they don't seem as daunting as they once did." With the help of a psychoactive drug, he was able to retire further and further from his mind's sight those images that were painful to him. He still saw their visible outlines, but his new mood was based on an altered perception of their image. He was no longer menaced by them because they had grown distant to him.

The same phenomenon can account for what Kramer calls "cosmetic psychopharmacology." Kramer reports with amazement how one of his female patients, after taking Prozac, changed from a social misfit into an accomplished coquette, capable of maneuvering smoothly from one man to the next, even of securing three dates in a single weekend. But is this any different from what alcohol might do for someone with similar hesitations? Is this really a "new self" courtesy of Prozac? Of course not. A woman wants to flirt with men, but her self-doubt tells her not to do so. The result is tension and unhappiness. So she takes alcohol in order to silence the critic within and feel "liberated." This is nothing new.

## Prozac nation

Yet despite the rather obvious nature of antidepressants, medical science studiously avoids putting antidepressants in the same category as alcohol and narcotics. It struggles to preserve the deceit of a special mood-matter link at the level of the neuronal junctions. Why is this so? Why does it bother to support the irrational notion that mood and matter share a common interface? To the degree that it is a conspiracy, it is one enjoined by our entire culture: People desperately want to believe in such a link; they want to believe that the cause of happiness is located in the physical world, and that happiness somehow comes about scientifically in the form of a pill. The promise of such a view is security and comfort.

First, to admit one's dependence on psychoactive drugs is to shield oneself from life's imponderables and unpredictability. If happiness is serotonin, and serotonin is happiness, then these drugs guarantee happiness, for one can take psychoactive drugs for years. It is with this attitude that people with mild depression might substitute the chance of real happiness with some semblance of happiness achieved through medication.

Second, to declare happiness a law of necessity allows science to emphasize the subcellular processes inside the brain at the expense of everything else. Science can say: "It is man's basic nature to want happiness, but if the natural desire for happiness is linked to the physical nature of his brain, it cannot be linked to culture, which varies from society to society. The search for happiness begins and ends in nature, and so there is no reason to go beyond science." By believing this to be true, people can put aside other approaches to coping with daily troubles—which is convenient, since these remedies, whether they involve talking to a friend or asking for divine guidance, are never a sure thing.

Third, the notion that happiness is a law of science appeals to human pride. If unhappiness is chemical or biological, along with its treatment, a person need not ask, "Why am I unhappy?" In the past, this question provoked serious introspection and self-examination, as the effort to cope with unhappiness merged with larger questions about life and existence. Religion and philosophy demanded that people see themselves as part of a larger whole and taught that happiness depended on more than self-satisfaction. But if happiness is a law of science, then one does not have to go through this humbling experience. Through drugs, one can find happiness as a single, isolated individual.

Fourth, and perhaps most crucial, depressed persons equate the pleasant mood evoked by psychoactive drugs with happiness, even though, in the depths of their hearts, they are not sure exactly what they feel. Still, people do not want to live a lie, and so they will accept their drug-induced "happiness" as the real thing only if they believe that science has truly uncovered the biology of happiness. And this is what the biogenic amine theory of matter and mood represents. It reassures people who take medication that their good feeling is indeed happiness.

For people suffering from clinical depression, the mental state produced by these drugs must be considered an improvement, and often, a necessary one. But for those people who suffer from unhappiness, perhaps because of stress or because they are in bad relationships, these drugs are nothing more than a shortcut to a particular mental state that they believe to be happiness but is not. . . .

Medical science should confine itself to the treatment of clinical depression, rather than extend itself into the realm of everyday unhappiness. Medical science "helps" unhappy people by clouding their thoughts, by making them less aware of the world, and by sapping their urge to see themselves in a true light. People medicated for everyday unhappiness gain inner peace, but they do so through a real decrement in consciousness.

# 4

# Medication and Psychosocial Treatment Help Many Schizophrenic Patients Recover

## National Institute of Mental Health

*The National Institute of Mental Health is an agency of the U.S. government that conducts research on mental illness.*

The majority of people with schizophrenia improve greatly when treated with antipsychotic drugs. Since 1990, a number of new medications have been introduced that are effective in treating the symptoms of schizophrenia, especially hallucinations, agitation, and delusions. One of the advantages of these new antipsychotic drugs is that they carry a lower risk of side effects than their predecessors. Although patients in the early phases of drug treatment may suffer from drowsiness, muscle spasms, dry mouth, or blurred vision, many of these side effects can by corrected by lowering the dosage or can be controlled by other medications. In addition, the newer drugs appear to have a lower long-term risk of producing tardive dyskinesia, a disorder in which one suffers from involuntary movements of the mouth, lips, tongue, and, occasionally, the trunk, arms, and legs. Contrary to popular myth, these antipsychotic medications do not produce a "high" that causes people to become addicted to them. In addition, they do not act as a "chemical straitjacket" that destroys an individual's volition or personality. Instead, they help people to function rationally in the world. However, people with schizophrenia require strict monitoring to reduce the chance of relapse that is more likely to occur when the dosages are incorrect or a patient stops taking the medication.

Antipsychotic medications have been available since the mid-1950s. They have greatly improved the outlook for individual patients.

National Institute of Mental Health, "Schizophrenia," *NIH Publication no. 99-3517, 1999.*

These medications reduce the psychotic symptoms of schizophrenia and usually allow the patient to function more effectively and appropriately. Antipsychotic drugs are the best treatment now available, but they do not "cure" schizophrenia or ensure that there will be no further psychotic episodes. The choice and dosage of medication can be made only by a qualified physician who is well trained in the medical treatment of mental disorders. The dosage of medication is individualized for each patient, since people may vary a great deal in the amount of drug needed to reduce symptoms without producing troublesome side effects.

The large majority of people with schizophrenia show substantial improvement when treated with antipsychotic drugs. Some patients, however, are not helped very much by the medications and a few do not seem to need them. It is difficult to predict which patients will fall into these two groups and to distinguish them from the large majority of patients who *do* benefit from treatment with antipsychotic drugs.

A number of new antipsychotic drugs (the so-called "atypical antipsychotics") have been introduced since 1990. The first of these, clozapine (Clozaril®), has been shown to be more effective than other antipsychotics, although the possibility of severe side effects—in particular, a condition called agranulocytosis (loss of the white blood cells that fight infection)—requires that patients be monitored with blood tests every one or two weeks. Even newer antipsychotic drugs, such as risperidone (Risperdal®) and olanzapine (Zyprexa®), are safer than the older drugs or clozapine, and they also may be better tolerated. They may or may not treat the illness as well as clozapine, however. Several additional antipsychotics are currently under development.

---

*[A] misconception about antipsychotic drugs is that they act as a kind of mind control.*

---

Antipsychotic drugs are often very effective in treating certain symptoms of schizophrenia, particularly hallucinations and delusions; unfortunately, the drugs may not be as helpful with other symptoms, such as reduced motivation and emotional expressiveness. Indeed, the older antipsychotics (which also went by the name of "neuroleptics"), medicines like haloperidol (Haldol®) or chlorpromazine (Thorazine®), may even produce side effects that resemble the more difficult to treat symptoms. Often, lowering the dose or switching to a different medicine may reduce these side effects; the newer medicines, including olanzapine (Zyprexa®), quetiapine (Seroquel®), and risperidone (Risperdal®), appear less likely to have this problem. Sometimes when people with schizophrenia become depressed, other symptoms can appear to worsen. The symptoms may improve with the addition of an antidepressant medication.

Patients and families sometimes become worried about the antipsychotic medications used to treat schizophrenia. In addition to concern about side effects, they may worry that such drugs could lead to addiction. However, antipsychotic medications do not produce a "high" (euphoria) or addictive behavior in people who take them.

Another misconception about antipsychotic drugs is that they act as a kind of mind control, or a "chemical straitjacket." Antipsychotic drugs used at the appropriate dosage do not "knock out" people or take away their free will. While these medications can be sedating, and while this effect can be useful when treatment is initiated particularly if an individual is quite agitated, the utility of the drugs is not due to sedation but to their ability to diminish the hallucinations, agitation, confusion, and delusions of a psychotic episode. Thus, antipsychotic medications should eventually help an individual with schizophrenia to deal with the world more rationally.

## How long should people with schizophrenia take antipsychotic drugs?

Antipsychotic medications reduce the risk of future psychotic episodes in patients who have recovered from an acute episode. Even with continued drug treatment, some people who have recovered will suffer relapses. Far higher relapse rates are seen when medication is discontinued. In most cases, it would not be accurate to say that continued drug treatment "prevents" relapses; rather, it reduces their intensity and frequency. The treatment of severe psychotic symptoms generally requires higher dosages than those used for maintenance treatment. If symptoms reappear on a lower dosage, a temporary increase in dosage may prevent a full-blown relapse.

Because relapse of illness is more likely when antipsychotic medications are discontinued or taken irregularly, it is very important that people with schizophrenia work with their doctors and family members to adhere to their treatment plan. *Adherence* to treatment refers to the degree to which patients follow the treatment plans recommended by their doctors. Good adherence involves taking prescribed medication at the correct dose and proper times each day, attending clinic appointments, and/or carefully following other treatment procedures. Treatment adherence is often difficult for people with schizophrenia, but it can be made easier with the help of several strategies and can lead to improved quality of life.

There are a variety of reasons why people with schizophrenia may not adhere to treatment. Patients may not believe they are ill and may deny the need for medication, or they may have such disorganized thinking that they cannot remember to take their daily doses. Family members or friends may not understand schizophrenia and may inappropriately advise the person with schizophrenia to stop treatment when he or she is feeling better. Physicians, who play an important role in helping their patients adhere to treatment, may neglect to ask patients how often they are taking their medications, or may be unwilling to accommodate a patient's request to change dosages or try a new treatment. Some patients report that side effects of the medications seem worse than the illness itself. Further, substance abuse can interfere with the effectiveness of treatment, leading patients to discontinue medications. When a complicated treatment plan is added to any of these factors, good adherence may become even more challenging.

Fortunately, there are many strategies that patients, doctors, and families can use to improve adherence and prevent worsening of the illness. Some antipsychotic medications, including haloperidol (Haldol®), fluphenazine (Prolixin®), perphenazine (Trilafon®) and others, are available in long-acting injectable forms that eliminate the need to take pills every day. A major goal of current research on treatments for schizophrenia is to develop a wider variety of long-acting antipsychotics, especially the newer agents with milder side effects, which can be delivered through injection. Medication calendars or pill boxes labeled with the days of the week can help patients and caregivers know when medications have or have not been taken. Using electronic timers that beep when medications should be taken, or pairing medication taking with routine daily events like meals, can help patients remember and adhere to their dosing schedule. Engaging family members in observing oral medication taking by patients can help ensure adherence. In addition, through a variety of other methods of adherence monitoring, doctors can identify when pill taking is a problem for their patients and can work with them to make adherence easier. It is important to help motivate patients to continue taking their medications properly.

In addition to any of these adherence strategies, patient and family education about schizophrenia, its symptoms, and the medications being prescribed to treat the disease is an important part of the treatment process and helps support the rationale for good adherence.

## What about side effects?

Antipsychotic drugs, like virtually all medications, have unwanted effects along with their beneficial effects. During the early phases of drug treatment, patients may be troubled by side effects such as drowsiness, restlessness, muscle spasms, tremor, dry mouth, or blurring of vision. Most of these can be corrected by lowering the dosage or can be controlled by other medications. Different patients have different treatment responses and side effects to various antipsychotic drugs. A patient may do better with one drug than another.

The long-term side effects of antipsychotic drugs may pose a considerably more serious problem. Tardive dyskinesia (TD) is a disorder characterized by involuntary movements most often affecting the mouth, lips, and tongue, and sometimes the trunk or other parts of the body such as arms and legs. It occurs in about 15 to 20 percent of patients who have been receiving the older, "typical" antipsychotic drugs for many years, but TD can also develop in patients who have been treated with these drugs for shorter periods of time. In most cases, the symptoms of TD are mild, and the patient may be unaware of the movements.

*Antipsychotic medications should eventually help an individual with schizophrenia to deal with the world.*

Antipsychotic medications developed in recent years all appear to have a much lower risk of producing TD than the older, traditional antipsychotics. The risk is not zero, however, and they can produce side effects of their own such as weight gain. In addition, if given at too high of a dose, the newer medications may lead to problems such as social withdrawal and symptoms resembling Parkinson's disease, a disorder that affects movement. Nevertheless, the newer antipsychotics are a significant advance in treatment, and their optimal use in people with schizophrenia is a subject of much current research.

## What about psychosocial treatments?

Antipsychotic drugs have proven to be crucial in relieving the psychotic symptoms of schizophrenia—hallucinations, delusions, and incoherence—but are not consistent in relieving the behavioral symptoms of the disorder. Even when patients with schizophrenia are relatively free of psychotic symptoms, many still have extraordinary difficulty with communication, motivation, self-care, and establishing and maintaining relationships with others. Moreover, because patients with schizophrenia frequently become ill during the critical career-forming years of life (e.g., ages 18 to 35), they are less likely to complete the training required for skilled work. As a result, many with schizophrenia not only suffer thinking and emotional difficulties, but lack social and work skills and experience as well.

It is with these psychological, social, and occupational problems that psychosocial treatments may help most. While psychosocial approaches have limited value for acutely psychotic patients (those who are out of touch with reality or have prominent hallucinations or delusions), they may be useful for patients with less severe symptoms or for patients whose psychotic symptoms are under control. Numerous forms of psychosocial therapy are available for people with schizophrenia, and most focus on improving the patient's social functioning—whether in the hospital or community, at home, or on the job. Some of these approaches are described here. Unfortunately, the availability of different forms of treatment varies greatly from place to place.

• *Rehabilitation*

Broadly defined, rehabilitation includes a wide array of non-medical interventions for those with schizophrenia. Rehabilitation programs emphasize social and vocational training to help patients and former patients overcome difficulties in these areas. Programs may include vocational counseling, job training, problem-solving and money management skills, use of public transportation, and social skills training. These approaches are important for the success of the community-centered treatment of schizophrenia, because they provide discharged patients with the skills necessary to lead productive lives outside the sheltered confines of a mental hospital.

• *Individual Psychotherapy*

Individual psychotherapy involves regularly scheduled talks between the patient and a mental health professional such as a psychiatrist, psychologist, psychiatric social worker, or nurse. The sessions may focus on current or past problems, experiences, thoughts, feelings, or relationships. By sharing experiences with a trained empathic person—talking about their world with someone outside it—individuals with schizophrenia may gradually come to understand more about themselves and their problems. They can also learn to sort out the real from the unreal and distorted. Recent studies indicate that supportive, reality-oriented, individual psychotherapy, and cognitive-behavioral approaches that teach coping and problem-solving skills, can be beneficial for outpatients with schizophrenia. However, psychotherapy is not a substitute for antipsychotic medication, and it is most helpful once drug treatment first has relieved a patient's psychotic symptoms.

- *Family Education*

Very often, patients with schizophrenia are discharged from the hospital into the care of their family; so it is important that family members learn all they can about schizophrenia and understand the difficulties and problems associated with the illness. It is also helpful for family members to learn ways to minimize the patient's chance of relapse—for example, by using different treatment adherence strategies—and to be aware of the various kinds of outpatient and family services available in the period after hospitalization. Family "psychoeducation," which includes teaching various coping strategies and problem-solving skills, may help families deal more effectively with their ill relative and may contribute to an improved outcome for the patient.

- *Self-Help Groups*

Self-help groups for people and families dealing with schizophrenia are becoming increasingly common. Although not led by a professional therapist, these groups may be therapeutic because members provide continuing mutual support as well as comfort in knowing that they are not alone in the problems they face. Self-help groups may also serve other important functions. Families working together can more effectively serve as advocates for needed research and hospital and community treatment programs. Patients acting as a group rather than individually may be better able to dispel stigma and draw public attention to such abuses as discrimination against the mentally ill.

Family and peer support and advocacy groups are very active and provide useful information and assistance for patients and families of patients with schizophrenia and other mental disorders.

# 5

# Medication May Hinder Recovery from Schizophrenia

## Robert Whitaker

*Robert Whitaker is the author of* Mad in America: Bad Science, Bad Medicine, and the Enduring Mistreatment of the Mentally Ill.

In the United States and other developed countries, people suffering from schizophrenia remain chronically ill because of the antipsychotic medication they are prescribed. In contrast, schizophrenic patients in poorer countries such as India and Nigeria have much higher rates of recovery because their treatment does not include such drugs. A 1998 study by University of Pennsylvania researchers reported that antipsychotic medications cause part of the brain to become enlarged and that this enlargement is associated with a worsening of schizophrenic symptoms. Some European physicians are seeking effective nondrug treatments for schizophrenia and are exploring treatments such as counseling and social support with some promising results. Clearly, U.S. psychiatrists need to reform the treatment offered to schizophrenics and find alternatives to antipsychotic medications.

The movie *A Beautiful Mind*, nominated for eight Academy Awards [in 2002], has brought welcome attention to the fact that people can and do recover from schizophrenia, a severely disabling disorder that affects about one in 100 Americans. Unfortunately, the film fabricates a critical detail of John Nash's recovery [John Nash is the main character who suffers from schizophrenia] and in so doing, obscures a question that should concern us all: Do the medications we use to treat schizophrenia promote long-term recovery—or hinder it? In the movie, Nash—just before he receives a Nobel Prize—speaks of taking "newer medications." The National Alliance for the Mentally Ill has praised the film's director, Ron Howard, for showing the "vital role of medication" in Nash's recovery. But as Sylvia Nasar notes in her biography of Nash, on which the movie is loosely based, this brilliant mathematician stopped taking anti-psychotic drugs in 1970 and slowly recovered over two decades. Nasar concluded that Nash's refusal to take drugs "may have been fortunate" because their deleterious effects "would have made his gentle re-entry into the world of mathematics a near impossibility."

---

*Long-term schizophrenia outcomes are much worse in the USA . . . than in poor [countries].*

---

His is just one of many such cases. Most Americans are unaware that the World Health Organization (WHO) has repeatedly found that long-term schizophrenia outcomes are much worse in the USA and other "developed" countries than in poor ones such as India and Nigeria, where relatively few patients are on anti-psychotic medications. In "undeveloped" countries, nearly two-thirds of schizophrenia patients are doing fairly well five years after initial diagnosis; about 40% have basically recovered. But in the USA and other developed countries, most patients become chronically ill. The outcome differences are so marked that WHO concluded that living in a developed country is a "strong predictor" that a patient never will fully recover.

## The myth of medication

There is more. In 1987, psychologist Courtenay Harding reported that a third of chronic schizophrenia patients released from Vermont State Hospital in the late 1950s completely recovered. Everyone in this "best-outcomes" group shared one common factor: All had weaned themselves from anti-psychotic medications. The notion that schizophrenics must spend a lifetime on these drugs, she concluded, is a "myth."

In 1994, Harvard Medical School researchers found that outcomes for U.S. schizophrenia patients had worsened during the past 20 years and were now no better than they were 100 years earlier, when therapy involved plunking patients into bathtubs for hours. And in 1998, University of Pennsylvania investigators reported that standard anti-psychotic medications cause a specific area of the brain to become abnormally enlarged and that this drug-induced enlargement is associated with a worsening of symptoms.

## Comprehensive care succeeds

All of this has led a few European physicians to explore non-drug alternatives. In Finland, doctors treat newly diagnosed schizophrenia patients with comprehensive care: counseling, social-support services and the selective use of anti-psychotic medications. Some patients do better on low doses of medication, and some without it. And they report great results: A majority of patients remain free of psychotic symptoms for extended periods and hold down jobs.

John Nash's recovery from schizophrenia is a moving story. But we are not well served when the movie fibs about the anti-psychotic drugs' role in his recovery. If anything, his story should inspire us to reconsider anti-psychotics' long-term efficacy with an honest, open mind. That would be a first step toward reforming our care—and if there is one thing we can conclude from the WHO studies, it is that reform is vitally needed. Perhaps then we could even hope that schizophrenia outcomes in this country would improve to the point that they were equal to those in poor countries such as India and Nigeria.

# 6

# Many Children Benefit from Psychiatric Medication

## Vidya Bhushan Gupta

*Vidya Bhushan Gupta is chief of developmental pediatrics at Metropolitan Hospital Center in New York. He is also an associate professor of clinical pediatrics at New York Medical College and a visiting associate research scientist at Columbia University.*

In recent years some determined lobbyists and the popular press have created hysteria over the purported dangers of Ritalin, a medication used to treat children for attention deficit disorder (ADD). In fact, the majority of children who are treated with Ritalin benefit from the drug. It helps them to decrease their impulsivity and hyperactivity and to improve their social behavior and attention. As a result, they also improve their academic performance. The side effects of Ritalin have been greatly exaggerated. The fear that Ritalin will make children into zombies is unjustified. It does not cause drowsiness or decrease mental abilities. Next, Ritalin does not cause children to become mindless robots who just follow orders. The drug simply helps children to overcome unproductive distraction that interferes with the achievement of their own goals. Despite popular reports, there is no evidence that Ritalin causes cancer or muscle twitches. Another myth about Ritalin is that it is an amphetamine that causes euphoria in children and leads them to become addicted to it. On the contrary, Ritalin is not an amphetamine and does not cause euphoria in the doses prescribed by physicians. Finally, Ritalin does not stunt children's growth, as has been erroneously reported.

Since time immemorial Man has been searching for a panacea—a drug—that will cure all maladies, physical and mental. Although the goal of a cure-all is as remote today as it was in antiquity, with the discovery of antibiotics and genetically and chemically engineered drugs in the twentieth century, the goal of a specific drug for each disease appears within reach. We do not have a magic pill for ADD [attention deficit disorder] yet, but, theoretically, it is a distinct possibility because ADD is, most likely, caused by a chemical imbalance. Indeed, about three-quarters of the children who are treated with medications for ADD benefit from them, whereas the majority of the children who are treated without medications continue to have significant problems. Drugs decrease impulsivity and motor restlessness and improve social behavior and attention, indirectly, improving academic performance. Better academic performance, in turn, improves self-esteem and social acceptance. Parent/child and teacher/child conflicts ameliorate as the child becomes more responsive to parents' and teachers' requests.

Although some religious groups and naturopaths take a strong exception to the "desecration of the body" by extraneous chemicals—especially those for a disease of the mind—taking an additional chemical is like adding a drop in the ocean of chemicals that make up the body. The human body is a soup of tens of thousands of chemicals, such as hormones, enzymes, and neurotransmitters. Almost every process in the body—from digesting the food that we eat to unfolding the genetic information that we inherit from our parents—is chemical. Each organ of the body is like a sea in this vast ocean, each with its own array of chemicals. Of the myriad chemicals that make up the human brain, neurotransmitters are the most important for moment-to-moment operations of the brain, because they carry the message of one nerve cell to another, as would a courier, across the cleft (technically called *synapse*) between the nerve cells. Every stimulus that our sensory organs receive, every thought that crosses our mind, every emotion that we feel stirs up this sea of neurotransmitters. Therefore, if a disorder occurs because of the deficiency or malfunction of a particular neurotransmitter, its rational treatment should include administering the neurotransmitter or medicines that increase its availability and reception at the synaptic cleft. That is exactly what the medications for ADD purport to do.

**First-line medications:** The first line of chemical defense against ADD is a group of medications called *psychostimulants*, a misnomer that has caused much misgiving in the lay press. These medications work in areas of the brain—such as the prefrontal cortex—that regulate attention, releasing dopamine from nerve cells and preventing its reuptake by the cells; thus increasing the levels of dopamine in the cleft between nerve cells. The foremost among the psychostimulants is methylphenidate (sold under the brand name of Ritalin by the drug company Ciba-Geigy, now Novartis), the most commonly prescribed medication for ADD. The others include the various salts of dextroamphetamine (sold as Dexedrine, Adderall, or Dextrostat) and pemoline sodium (sold as Cylert).

• **Methylphenidate (Ritalin).** This drug was approved by the Federal Drug Administration (FDA) in 1955 under the brand name Ritalin for the pharmaceutical company Ciba-Geigy, now Novartis. Ciba-Geigy's patent expired in 1996, and now many companies make the generic form of the drug. Methylphenidate is available as 5-, 10-, and 20-mg tablets. Long-acting tablets are available in 20-mg strength as sustained-release (SR) tablets and in 10-, 18-, 20-, and 36-mg extended-release tablets. A liquid form is not available. The regular form acts only for four hours, while the sustained-release form acts from six to eight hours. The tablet should be swallowed whole and should preferably be taken thirty minutes before eating. Although pharmacists caution not to divide the tablet, no significant loss of potency occurs if it is. Similarly, no substantial loss of potency occurs if the medication is taken with or after food. Although the FDA does not approve the use of methylphenidate for children under the age of six years old, this caution simply means that data substantiating the effectiveness and safety of Ritalin are not available in children below the age of six years old. The Federal Drug and Cosmetic Act does not limit the manner in which a physician uses it. In fact, Ritalin has been given to children as young as four years old without any problems. . . .

## Side-effects hysteria—is it justified?

Contrary to the frenetic propaganda of the anti-Ritalin lobby, methylphenidate is a safe medication. Russell Barkley, a nationally renowned researcher in the field of ADD, reported in 1990 that, out of eighty-three school-age children who received Ritalin, only three had to discontinue it because of side effects. Seventeen side effects alleged to be associated with the administration of Ritalin were meticulously monitored by parents in this study, using a zero-to-nine rating scale. Similar results have been reported for preschool children. Researchers at the University of Ottawa, Ontario, Canada, noted, in cognitive tests, improvements in attention and reduction of impulsivity with methylphenidate in preschool children. The children's ability to work more productively also showed improvement.

---

*About three-quarters of the children who are treated with medications for ADD benefit from them.*

---

Passions against Ritalin are also abetted by the long list of adverse effects given in the *Physician's Desk Reference (PDR)*. This document, published by the Medical Economics Company in collaboration with drug manufacturers, is now widely available to practitioners and consumers through the Internet and provides an "exact copy of the product's government-approved labeling" for all prescription drugs available on the market. The Code of Federal Regulations further requires that "any relevant warnings, hazards, contraindications, side effects, and precautions" be included in the *PDR* content and must be the "same in language and emphasis" as the product label that has been approved. Because the intent of the law is to inform the consumer of all possible adverse effects— even if they are infrequent—the cautions and side effects listed in the *PDR* can be alarming. However, one should compare the frequency of side effects in those receiving the medication with the frequency of side effects in a similar group of individuals not receiving the medication. If an adverse effect occurs more frequently in those taking a particular medication, only then should it be attributed to the medication. Every association is not causal. Many of the side effects reported to the FDA's Spontaneous Reporting System can occur by chance and not necessarily due to Ritalin. Many of the adverse effects of Ritalin listed in the PDR are very infrequent and cause minuscule inconvenience as compared with the pervasive dysfunction that ADD causes. Or, in other words, the risks of taking Ritalin are much smaller than the benefit that accrues from it.

According to the *PDR*, the possible side effects of Ritalin include loss of appetite, difficulty in sleeping (insomnia), headache, stomachache, tics, agitation, dizziness, sadness (melancholia), unhappiness (dysphoria), proneness to crying, decreased linear growth, abdominal pain, palpitations, increase of heart rate and blood pressure, skin rashes and itching, and weight loss. However, only appetite suppression, lack of sleep, stomachache, headache, and dizziness are reported to occur more often in those receiving methyphenidate as compared with those not receiving it. Rebound effects—such as, ravenous appetite and irritability—which occur as the effect of the drug wanes in the evenings, can be controlled by adjusting the frequency and dose of the medication. Stomachaches and headaches are temporary and decrease after a few days. The effect on appetite can be mitigated by administering methylphenidate with or after food. Insomnia does not occur if the medicine is not administered in late evening.

---

*The risks of taking Ritalin are much smaller than the benefit that accrues from it.*

---

According to a group of researchers at the Royal Children's Hospital, Melbourne, Australia, many of the alleged side effects are indeed "preexisting characteristics of children with ADHD [attention deficit and hyperactivity disorder—a term used interchangeably with ADD]." Similarly researchers at the University of British Columbia, Vancouver, Canada, found that many side effects reported by parents and teachers are similar to the symptoms of ADD.

Palpitations and increased blood pressure are so uncommon in therapeutic doses that the American Heart Association in its seventy-first session in Boston, Massachusetts, declared that no cardiac monitoring is required for Ritalin. Intravenous injection of high doses of methylphenidate in experimental animals has been reported to produce a few microscopic changes in the heart muscle, but the clinical significance of these changes is unknown.

## No, Ritalin does not make children zombies

The fear that methylphenidate will make a child a zombie is absolutely baseless. Methylphenidate neither causes drowsiness nor decreases mental abilities. Researchers at McGill University in Canada reported a positive effect of methylphenidate on measures of mental flexibility and problem-solving abilities. A very small fraction of children taking Ritalin appear sad and cry excessively. Obviously, such children are not suitable candidates for Ritalin.

## No, Ritalin does not cause "robotic conformity"

A child taking Ritalin follows class rules rather than his impulses. This improves his academic performance and social behavior. Whereas a child with ADD constantly craves reinforcement and approval, the effort of a child receiving Ritalin becomes goal-directed and independent of rewards. Methylphenidate improves persistence by enhancing the processes that maintain effort over time. Yes, a child taking Ritalin loses unproductive spontaneity—spontaneity that disrupts others and interferes with his own goals. And, yes, he conforms to societal rules. But he does not become a robot, a mindless creature that just follows orders.

## Ritalin and cancer

Ciba-Geigy (now Novartis), the pharmaceutical company that patented Ritalin, conducted trials on animals and found no evidence that Ritalin causes cancer, even if it was used for long periods of time. Researchers at the National Institute of Environmental Health Sciences administered a wide range of methylphenidate doses to rats and mice over a number of years, but did not find any increase in cancers in rats. In fact, they reported less than the expected rate of cancers in rats taking methylphenidate. However, a slight increase in benign tumors of the liver and increased liver weights was observed in mice at a high dose. An increase in hepatoblastomas [liver cancer] was also seen in high-dose male mice. Such high doses are rarely used to treat ADD. The authors concluded that "epidemiologic studies of methylphenidate have found no evidence of a carcinogenic effect in humans and like our findings in rats, report a less than expected rate of cancers in patients taking methylphenidate."

## Ritalin and tics

It is generally believed that methylphenidate can induce muscle twitches and spasms, called tics. Tics result in sudden blinking, jerking of the hands or shrugging of the shoulders, or making faces. However, this happens only in those children who have a history of tics or whose families have another member who has tics. In other words, Ritalin can induce a latent tendency for tics, but it does not induce tics in those who do not have a predisposition to them. In fact, in children in whom tics were due to hyperactivity, methylphenidate actually improved tics. Researchers at the Hospital for Sick Children in Toronto, Canada, found that Ritalin did not precipitate or exacerbate tics.

## Ritalin is not "speed"

The misnomer "psychostimulant" perpetuates a myth that Ritalin is an amphetamine—or speed. Chemically, Ritalin (methylphenidate) is a piperidine, whereas amphetamine is methylphenethylamine. In the doses prescribed by physicians, methylphenidate does not cause euphoria or enhance performance. Calling Ritalin "kiddie cocaine" is hyperbole. However, the problems and risks mount significantly when Ritalin is abused by taking it in high doses and through abnormal routes. . . .

## Ritalin and suppression of growth

The issue of growth suppression by methylphenidate was examined by researchers at the Massachusetts General Hospital, in Boston. The growth of

124 children with ADD was compared with that of 109 controls. A small difference in height was noted between the ADD and non-ADD children through mid-adolescence, but it was unrelated to the use of methylphenidate. Moreover, by late adolescence this difference disappeared. Dr. Peter R. Breggin, author of *Talking Back to Ritalin*—in which he suggests that Ritalin suppresses growth—contradicts himself by citing Yudofsky and colleagues, who, according to him, admit that growth lag induced by Ritalin is temporary "in most cases."

---

*Ritalin has been given to children as young as four years old without any problems.*

---

A multicenter study group sponsored by the National Institute of Mental Health has concluded that methylphenidate is superior to psychosocial interventions in simple ADD. The study included 579 children between the ages of seven and nine years at six medical centers across the U. S. and Canada: New York State Psychiatric Institute, Duke University, University of California (in Berkeley and in Irvine), University of Pittsburgh, and McGill University (Montreal, Canada). The study is being hailed as a landmark that, according to Dr. James T. McCracken, the director of child and adolescent psychiatry at the Neuropsychiatric Institute of the University of California at Los Angeles, should put the Ritalin controversy to rest. Methylphenidate and dextroamphetamine are the safest and most effective treatments for ADD. Dextroamphetamine has been used for over fifty years and Ritalin for over forty years, both without significant long-term adverse effects.

# 7

# Doctors Are Overprescribing Psychiatric Medication to Children

## Lawrence H. Diller

*Lawrence H. Diller is a behavioral pediatrician and the author of* Running on Ritalin: A Physician Reflects on Children, Society, and Performance in a Pill.

Doctors are prescribing psychiatric drugs to children in unprecedented numbers for conditions ranging from attention deficit disorder (ADD) to depression and anxiety. Approximately 5 million American children, some as young as two, are being given potentially dangerous psychiatric drugs alone and in combination, including Ritalin, Prozac, Zoloft, Wellbutrin, and Dexadrine. One of the disturbing aspects of this development is that only two of the most frequently prescribed medications, Luvox and Zoloft, have been approved by the FDA for psychiatric use in children. The studies of the newer medications have only looked at the efficacy and side effects of the drugs over the course of a few months and have not investigated their effects on children's growth and development. Although research has shown that the results of an adult drug study cannot be generalized to children, doctors cite such adult medication trials to justify prescribing some drugs to children. Further, children are wrongly being prescribed powerful psychotropic drugs for "conditions" such as out-of-control behavior that might be the result of family problems or problems at school rather than a mental illness. The trend in medicating children is being propelled by the profit-driven pharmaceutical industry.

I've practiced behavioral pediatrics since 1978 in Walnut Creek, Calif., an affluent suburb of San Francisco. I have evaluated and treated more than 2,000 children who struggle with behavior and performance at home or at school. In 1999 alone, I wrote more than 400 prescriptions for Ritalin or a similar stimulant. I am not against prescribing psychiatric medication to children.

But I've become increasingly uneasy with the role I play and the readiness of families and doctors to medicate children.

I recently obtained some information from the National Disease and Therapeutic Index of IMS Health that adds to my uneasiness about the number of children taking psychiatric drugs in the United States.

IMS Health is to drug companies what the A.C. Nielsen company is to television networks. The pharmaceutical industry relies on it to report on the latest trends in medication usage. The company recently surveyed changes in doctors' use of psychiatric drugs on children between 1995 and 1999 and found stimulant drug use is up 23 percent; the use of Prozac-like drugs for children under 18 is up 74 percent; in the 7–12 age group it's up 151 percent; for kids 6 and under it's up a surprising 580 percent. For children under 18, the use of mood stabilizers other than lithium is up 40-fold, or 4,000 percent and the use of new antipsychotic medications such as Risperdal has grown nearly 300 percent.

---

*Diagnosing bipolar disorder in children as young as 3 has become the latest rage.*

---

Approximately 5 million American children take a psychiatric drug today. Based on production/use quotas maintained by the Drug Enforcement Administration and national physician practice surveys, it's possible to say with confidence that nearly 4 million children took the stimulant drug Ritalin, or its equivalent, in 1998.

Stimulants such as Ritalin have been used for more than 60 years to treat hyperactivity and inattentiveness in children. Since 1990, however, psychiatric drug use for children has broadened considerably. There are more drugs and they are being used for more purposes. Ritalin is now prescribed for children as young as 2 and 3. A recent Michigan survey of Medicaid children found a few hundred toddlers taking stimulants and other psychiatric drugs. A study in the *Journal of the American Medical Association* confirmed this trend in children of privately insured families.

Medicines originally developed and tested to treat depression in adults, such as the well-known Prozac (now in liquid form for easy pediatric administration), Paxil and Zoloft, but also Wellbutrin, Effexor and Serzone, are now being employed for a wide range of children's behavioral problems. Medications originally developed to treat blood pressure, such as clonidine (Catapress) and its longer-acting relative, Tenex, are also being used for behavioral management.

## A child on three psychiatric medications

Pierre, 8-year-old Bobby's father, pleaded with me to evaluate his son. Bobby was on three different psychiatric medications. Pierre and Bobby's mother, Carol, had bitterly divorced and had been fighting since Bobby was 2. Bobby had had problems at school since kindergarten. Teachers described him as distractible, hyperactive, slow to learn and with few friends. But his behavior at home, especially with his mother, posed the biggest headaches. He defied Carol and flew into violent rages, hitting and trying to bite her. Time outs were ineffective because he would either escape from his room or completely trash it.

Pierre admitted that he had seen this kind of behavior from Bobby only three or four times over the past three years. But at Carol's, Bobby had major temper tantrums at least weekly. Carol took Bobby to a child therapist when he was 4. The therapist thought Bobby might have "ADD"—attention deficit disorder or, properly, ADHD (H for hyperactivity). She also thought he was depressed because of the divorce. Weekly play-therapy sessions for Bobby continued for three years and Carol sometimes got advice from the therapist on how to handle Bobby.

Pierre only met the therapist once. He acknowledged he'd never been a big fan of therapy and questioned its value. Carol had been a psychiatric patient for much of their 17-year marriage. She suffered from serious bouts of depression and took Prozac, the well-known antidepressant, and Ativan, a medication for anxiety much like Valium.

Bobby's pediatrician started him at age 5 on Ritalin, the best-known stimulant for ADHD, because the boy kept getting up from circle time and twice ran out of the classroom at school. Later he was switched to a very similar stimulant medication, Dexedrine. Bobby's acting out and impulsiveness continued, so Carol took him to a child psychiatrist who added the drug Wellbutrin to his regimen, thinking that Bobby's irritability might be a sign of depression. (Wellbutrin has been used primarily to treat depression in adults, but has also been employed for a variety of other problems from anorexia nervosa to stopping smoking.) The Wellbutrin did not make much of a difference and after two months was stopped.

---

*No other society prescribes psychoactive medications to children the way we do.*

---

Bobby's problem persisted. At Carol's his bedtime would begin at 8:30 and at 11 Bobby was still up, getting out of bed, pestering his mother for water or food and driving her "crazy." Another medication, Anafranil, was prescribed to help him fall asleep. (Anafranil was originally used in adult depression and obsessive-compulsive disorder, a condition of unwanted recurrent thoughts and compulsive behaviors like repetitive hand washing. But it often was too sedating for most people to tolerate.) Bobby fell asleep faster when he took this pill. Pierre, who in general had fewer problems with Bobby, only occasionally gave him this medication.

Bobby was 7 when Carol took him to a private psychiatric clinic well known for its controversial use of brain scans for psychiatric diagnosis and its liberal use of psychoactive medications. Bobby, now getting bigger, had stabbed another child with a pencil. No brain scan was done but the psychiatrist said that Bobby suffered from bipolar disorder, the current name for manic depression, and should take yet another drug. This fifth medication, Neurontin, originally approved as an anticonvulsant, more recently had been categorized felicitously as a "mood stabilizer." The psychiatrist said this medication would help Bobby control his episodes of rage and prevent a further worsening of his symptoms.

When I first met Bobby he took Dexedrine in the morning, Neurontin three times a day and Anafranil at night only before bedtime. He took 12 pills a day when he stayed with his mother. At his father's, he usually skipped the Dexedrine and Anafranil, especially on weekends. Pierre was afraid to stop the Neurontin because he had been told that Bobby might experience headache and irritability if that medication were abruptly discontinued.

Bobby was a very unhappy, angry boy caught in a web of strained emotions and loyalties between his parents. He was not an easy child to raise, especially for his mother, who had her own problems with depression. Bobby's story is disturbing not for its uniqueness but for how it represents a growing trend in the U.S.—young children are being given essentially untested and potentially dangerous psychotropic drugs alone and in combination in greater volume than ever before.

## Diagnosing bipolar disorder in very young children

Diagnosing bipolar disorder in children as young as 3 has become the latest rage. It justifies using a host of meds to treat very difficult-to-manage, unhappy children. The old-line drug, lithium, has been replaced by newer, untested (in children) mood stabilizers like Neurontin or Depakote as a first-choice intervention for pediatric "manic depression." Finally, a new class of anti-psychotic medications—the most popular these days is Risperdal—is heralded as the ultimately effective treatment for a number of diagnoses whose common features are not hallucinations or psychosis, but severe acting-out behaviors.

No one knows precisely how many children are taking these non-stimulant medications. The most recent survey of physicians' practices had 1.5 million children taking an anti-depressant in 1996. Most were teenagers (girls are the majority), but more than 200,000 children under 12 are also prescribed an antidepressant. Other data tells us that rates of antidepressant use since 1996 continue to rise. For example, 150,000 prescriptions for clonidine were written for children in 1996. More than 100,000 children take "mood-stabilizing" drugs for purported bipolar disorder. Again, most are teens (here boys predominate) but it's being advised that children as young as 3 take these drugs. More than 200,000 children receive anti-psychotic medications, mostly to control unruly behavior rather than to treat hallucinations or other symptoms of schizophrenia. The number of children combining two or more psychoactive drugs is unknown. Combined pharmacotherapy (known pejoratively as polypharmacy) has been strongly endorsed by leading research groups as the sensible approach to treating the co-morbid, or multiple occurring, diagnoses common in "high problem resistant behavior" children. Some doctors call it prescribing by "symptom chasing."

## The United States prescribes 80 percent of the world's stimulants

No other society prescribes psychoactive medications to children the way we do. We use 80 percent of the world's stimulants such as Ritalin. Only Canada comes close to our rates, using half, per capita, the amounts we do. Europe and industrialized Asia use one-10th of what we do. Psychiatrists in those countries are perplexed and worried about trends in America. The use of psychoactive drugs other than Ritalin for preteen children is virtually unheard of outside this country.

In my practice of behavioral pediatrics I regularly meet children under 13 on two psychiatric medications. A 5-year-old girl troubled by fears had tried eight different psychoactive drugs over the year before she saw me. I met the mother of a 29-month-old boy who wanted me to prescribe medication. I didn't, but later I learned the boy was getting lithium, Zoloft and Risperdal from another doctor.

Is this cutting-edge treatment or an outrage? I'm not sure. But with three or four exceptions, none of these drugs, alone or in combination, has been shown to be effective for a specific psychiatric condition in children. Outside of the stimulants and old-line anti-psychotic group, only two of the most frequently prescribed medications, Luvox and Zoloft, have been studied sufficiently to obtain the Food and Drug Administration's approval for psychiatric use in children. Only a handful more have been examined systematically to eliminate the placebo effect, which has a particularly powerful influence in psychiatric conditions and in children. None of the newer medications has been studied beyond a few months for efficacy or side effects, and no one has looked at their effects on children's growth and development.

Until recently the recondite and rarified worlds of academic child psychiatry and psychology have largely supported the increased use of these medications. Joseph Biederman, chief of Harvard's pediatric psychopharmacology clinic, hails the increased use of psychiatric drugs in children as evidence "that child psychiatry is finally catching up to adult psychiatry" in psychopharmacological practice.

Other leaders in the field of child psychiatry are not as sanguine. Michael Jellinek, who as the head of child psychiatry at Harvard is effectively Biederman's boss, and Peter Jensen, who recently stepped down as director of child and adolescent research of the National Institutes of Mental Health, have both publicly worried whether physicians' prescribing practices for children have outstripped their scientific substantiation. They are also concerned that not enough is being done about the world these troubled children live in.

## The growing belief that mental illness is biological

What makes America so different from the rest of the world in how it views and treats children's emotional and behavioral problems? Perhaps no other profession fell so completely under the sway of Freudian ideas as American psychiatry and psychology did in the first 60 years of the 20th century. Yet by the late 1960s critics both within and outside of American psychiatry had doubts about psychoanalysis as a science and as an effective treatment. In the 1950s drugs like lithium, Thorazine and Elavil, found to be useful in alleviating psychiatric symptoms, further challenged the Freudian hegemony on psychiatric thinking and practice in this country.

By the 1970s research and academic psychiatrists fomented an internal revolution culminating in 1980 with the publication of the third edition of the Diagnostic and Statistical Manual of Mental Disorders (DSM-III). The DSM III replaced the old Freudian diagnoses, which were based on traumatic childhood experience, with etiologically neutral lists of symptoms collected into supposedly definable syndromes. DSM III was meant only to be descriptive and used primarily for research. Few outside of an inner circle of research psychiatrists knew of a paragraph in the introduction, deleted at the last moment (ostensibly to maintain etiological neutrality), that said the presumptive cause of most of the disorders listed was biological, that is, the result of heredity or a chemical imbalance.

---

*With so many adults taking a drug for mood, it didn't take long for the primary drug for children's behavior, Ritalin, to zoom in use.*

---

It really didn't matter what was written, because over the next 10 years American academic psychiatry shifted 180 degrees from blaming Johnny's mother for all his problems to blaming Johnny's brain and genes.

The introduction of Prozac in the late 1980s cemented America's belief in the biological basis for abnormal behavior. Prozac was no more effective than earlier antidepressants but had less severe side effects, which allowed greater numbers of less severely disabled people to continue to take the drug. A logic developed that if a drug improved behavior, the problems must be biologically based. No one speaks of headache as an "aspirin deficiency" even though the drug relieves the symptoms. Nevertheless terms like "chemical imbalance" became increasingly fashionable in explaining problem behavior.

Media exaggeration of scientific findings contributed to the revolution. The acceptance of Prozac made taking a psychotropic drug no longer taboo; it became the topic of dinner-party conversation. Nearly one in 10 Americans has taken Prozac or one of its close drug relatives. With so many adults taking a drug for mood, it didn't take long for the primary drug for children's behavior, Ritalin, to zoom in use.

Ritalin production and use for the treatment of ADHD rose by more than 700 percent between 1991 and 1998. Amphetamine production also used for ADHD initially lagged but has tripled in use since 1996. Trade amphetamine (primarily Adderall) surpassed trade Ritalin prescriptions in 1998, a testament primarily to the marketing success of the manufacturers of Adderall. As Prozac opened the door for Ritalin use in children, Ritalin itself ushered in a new "better children through chemistry" age in our country. At least Ritalin had been the most studied of pediatric drugs, though only a handful of the thousands of studies look at patients other than boys or monitor the children beyond a couple of weeks. Meanwhile research on other psychotropic drugs for use in children has been limited. Until recently, funding for studies of psychiatric medication in children was meager by adult comparisons. Questions about children's rights and consent to participate in studies raised thorny ethical issues, and the pharmaceutical industry did not believe there was much of a market for these drugs in children and so it did not fund studies. Ironically, the new belief in a robust market for psychotropics in children has fueled a host of pending studies of different drugs for different child psychiatric conditions.

## New studies on pediatric psychopharmacology

The community of pediatric psychopharmacology researchers is rather small; Biederman's Harvard program has been arguably the most productive and influential. His work stands as prototypic of children's psychiatric research under the DSM (now in its fourth edition) and demonstrates how a drug becomes established in the pediatric psychiatric pharmacopea. His research has won awards and his professional publications are prolific.

Biederman's group demonstrated in the late 1980s that the tricyclic antidepressants (their chemical structure contains three "rings") imipramine and desipramine, abandoned as a treatment for childhood depression because studies had shown them to be ineffective, could be used in high doses to successfully treat children with ADHD who had failed to respond to stimulants. In 1996, the Harvard clinic published a paper that said that 23 percent of their ADHD children also "had" bipolar disorder. (Most child psychiatrists believed manic depression to be a rare disorder in children.)

The Harvard group had always found higher rates of co-occurrence or "co-morbidity" of other disorders in their ADHD patients, but this rate of bipolar disease in children astonished the world of academic child psychiatry.

Biederman further claimed he could diagnose manic depression in children as young as 3. Few of these children demonstrated the classic signs of mania, euphoria or grandiosity. They did not have distinct periods of several weeks or months between their highs and lows. These children could cycle on a daily basis. They were very angry, very irritable kids.

Few of these kids were crazy. They could distinguish reality as long as they weren't enraged. They were very unhappy and very difficult to control. But Biederman felt that children diagnosed as bipolar could be saved from a lifetime of antisocial behavior and substance abuse by aggressively treating them with medication.

---

*"Ritalin is for irritable and irritating children while lithium is for very irritable and very irritating children."*

---

The presumed hereditary and biochemical nature of bipolar disorder would justify the use of a new class of drugs known as mood stabilizers: lithium, Depakote, Neurontin—all drugs with far more serious short- and long-term side effects than Ritalin.

The response from other academic researchers was mixed. Debate goes on in the professional journals over the definition and frequency of bipolar disorder in children. One psychiatrist commented cynically that "Ritalin is for irritable and irritating children while lithium is for very irritable and very irritating children." The practical effect, though, of the announcement of this new interpretation of pediatric bipolar disorder, was that these medications began to be used in very young children without even short-term evidence of their effectiveness and safety.

Of late, the new anti-psychotic drug, Risperdal, has been touted by the Biederman group as more effective than mood stabilizers in controlling the symptoms of bipolar children. Risperdal's ascendancy as the drug of choice has not been slowed by a different set of more serious disabling side effects.

## The FDA's process for approving drugs

How should drugs properly be studied for use in children? Only two of the newer psychotropic drugs have been approved by the FDA for the treatment of a psychiatric condition in children. Paxil and Luvox, both variations of Prozac, have proved effective in clinical trials required by the FDA for the treatment of pediatric obsessive compulsive disorder (OCD). No other medication, as yet, has met FDA approval. Several drug trials in children, actively supported by the pharmaceutical industry, are under way.

Once a drug is approved for use by the FDA for the treatment of a specific medical condition, a doctor can legally prescribed it "off label" for any purpose. Virtually every other med used to treat children's behavior is prescribed this way. Off-label use of medicines in pediatrics is common, but nowhere more so than in psychiatric medications. Physicians are constrained only by their own judgment and ethics. Local hospital and medical boards usually do little to interfere with doctors' preferences for treatment.

Most of the drugs used to treat children's emotional problems first became available after they met the FDA's standards for approval in psychiatric clinical trials in adults. A few were initially approved for use in adults for other medical conditions: Depakote and Neurontin for control of seizures, clonidine for blood pressure.

The typical path to the widespread use of any of these drugs for children begins with a report of a single child's response to a drug, usually as a letter in one of the professional journals. Journal editors explicitly state their openness to these kinds of "case" reports and more critical peer review scrutiny is omitted. The report will generate other letters until a series of cases are reported in which everyone—the kids, parents and doctors—knows what drug the child is taking.

Such studies are notorious for creating expectations of both positive and unwanted placebo effects. In the only study demonstrating the effectiveness of Prozac in children when the patients and doctors didn't know which pill was taken, 60 percent of the improvement in depressive symptoms was attributed to the placebo effect.

The Super Bowl of drug testing, which supposedly can distinguish between the actual effects of the active ingredients of a medication and placebo, is called the double-blind randomized control study (DBRCS). In a DBRCS neither the family nor doctor knows whether the child is getting the medication or an identical capsule filled with an inert ingredient. Only the pharmacist who prepares the medication knows which capsule contains the drug to be tested.

Patients are carefully screened for the psychiatric condition to be treated and then are randomly selected to receive either the real drug or the placebo. The children are monitored by their parents and doctors for improvements and side effects; along with benefits coming from placebo, many children complain of unwanted effects like headache and stomachache while taking placebos. After a pre-determined period it is revealed who took the drug and who took the the placebo. Only then does one learn the "real" vs. "believed" effects of the drug.

Such DBRCS are expensive; until recently, pediatric psychopharmacology researchers have been limited by low funds for their studies. Those few DBRCSs that had been run usually included only enough children, usually fewer than 100, to generate the likelihood of a statistically significant difference between drug and placebo required for scientific journal publication, but not enough for FDA approval.

But with only scores of children assessed, drugs like Prozac, imipramine, clonidine and Wellbutrin have come to be prescribed for hundreds of thousands of children. Research with imipramine demonstrated that adult drug studies do not necessarily correspond to effects in children. Nonetheless, adult medication trials are regularly invoked to justify the use of those same agents in children.

Calls for increased funding for pediatric psychopharmacology research are ubiquitous within the child mental-health community. The pharmaceutical industry, which now sees a children's market large enough to justify the expense, is funding several large studies, hoping to obtain FDA approval for the tested drugs.

On the other hand, studies on psychosocial interventions provide no similar profit-driven initiative for investigation. The much lower funding for this kind of research comes primarily from government. However, with the profit-motive incentive to develop new drugs and the real-life pressures to medicate children these days, there is ever-increasing pressure to medicate. When all you've got is a hammer, everything starts to look like a nail.

# 8

# Psychologists Should Be Allowed to Prescribe Psychiatric Drugs

## Robert Sternberg

*Robert Sternberg is the president of the American Psychological Association. He is also a professor of psychology and education at Yale University and director of the university's Pace Center for Child Development. He is the author of* Off Track *and* Our Labeled Children.

Legislation to grant properly trained psychologists the right to prescribe medication should be passed. Psychologists are committed to providing the best treatment they can and need to have the option of prescribing drugs as a supplemental therapy to patients who will benefit from them. Most psychotropic medicines are prescribed by physicians with little training in psychology. Patients who are treated by such physicians lose the benefit of working with a psychologist who can offer psychological therapy to complement the drug treatment.

As an academic who specializes in learning abilities and disabilities, I am not often asked to confront the issue of prescription privileges for practicing psychologists. Nevertheless, the issue has stared me in the face several times lately. Hence, I have been unable to avoid it. First, as the coauthor of two books on learning disabilities (*Off Track* and *Our Labeled Children*), as well as the coeditor of another book (*Perspectives on Learning Disabilities*), I am frequently asked by the media and others about drug-related issues, such as prescription of ritalin and other drugs used to treat ADHD [attention deficit hyperactivity disorder]. Second, the Center I direct—the Center for the Psychology of Abilities, Competencies, and Expertise at Yale—is opening a practice unit, so any issue that confronts practicing psychologists now is confronting us. Third, as a candidate for the presidency of the American Psychological Association [Sternberg was elected to serve as president for the 2003 term], I have found that I need to take a stand on such an important issue. Fourth, these days, when so much is at stake because of the insidious spread of managed [health] care, any psychologist, practicing or otherwise, needs to be aware of the major issues confronting all of us today. But the issue came to a head recently when I was asked by the Connecticut State Psychological Association to testify in the Connecticut State Legislature regarding prescription privileges for psychologists. The time had come to do the research and take an informed position. I would do so in what I believe to be a fairly impartial way, because the issue does not directly affect me: I do not myself have a professional practice and so stand little to gain personally with regard to how the issue is resolved.

After investigating the issue, I have concluded that, despite all its complexity, the issue should be resolved in favor of passing legislation to permit properly trained psychologists to prescribe drugs. I therefore decided to testify. The hearing was very informative, not only with respect to what those in favor had to say, but with respect to what those in opposition had to say. I think the arguments in favor of prescription privileges are straightforward. I believe five arguments predominate.

*Treating the whole person with all means at one's disposal.* First, psychologists need to be able to treat the whole person. Research in health psychology has made increasingly clear that psychological and physiological systems are in continual interaction with each other. For example, psychological stress can lead to adverse physical-health outcomes, whereas psychological well-being can lead to favorable health outcomes. Similarly, bad physical health can lead to depression, anxiety, and other mental conditions, whereas good physical health can promote psychological wellness. Because of the constant interactions between the psychological and physical systems, a combination of psychological therapy with drugs potentially can make good sense.

*Rendering the best treatment of which one is capable.* Second, psychologists are pledged to do the very best they can in treating those who seek help. Some psychologists may believe that the best way for them to treat psychological conditions is with the available armamentarium of psychological methods of therapy. But other psychologists may believe that drugs can serve as a meaningful supplement to psychological treatment. In order for these psychologists to do what they are pledged to do, they ought to have the option of using drugs as a supplement to therapy.

---

*With proper training, psychologists can competently and successfully prescribe drugs.*

---

*The physician as an alternative.* Third, most prescriptions for psychoactive medications are made not by psychiatrists, but by physicians with fairly minimal training in psychology. These physicians may choose to treat patients in the only way they know how—using the medical model. Their patients thereby lose the benefit of psychological therapy to complement the drug treatment. Psychologists are much more likely, in my experience, to recognize the complementarity of the two kinds of treatment than are many physicians.

*Success has already been demonstrated.* Fourth, as I learned at the hearing, the Army has had a unit of practicing psychologists who have been trained to prescribe drugs. The unit has been highly successfully in prescribing drugs for thousands of people in need. These psychologists have shown that, with proper training, psychologists can competently and successfully prescribe drugs.

*Professional and financial incentives.* Fifth, from the point of view of many psychologists, there are good financial reasons to learn how to prescribe drugs. Everyone knows how the scourge of managed care has cut deeply into psychologists' professional options as well as their incomes. Many psychologists therefore have strong professional and financial incentives to learn all of the techniques possible to increase their desirability as care-givers to people in need. For some of them, prescription drugs provide one route to gaining the attention of people in need.

---

*Psychologists are those who are best trained to treat psychological problems.*

---

Psychologists are those who are best trained to treat psychological problems. Why should they not have all possible means at their disposal to render treatment?

A battalion of medical doctors, including psychiatrists, appeared at the Connecticut State hearing to speak in opposition to prescription privileges for psychologists. Many psychologists, too, oppose prescription privileges. I was therefore particularly interested in the kinds of arguments that were mustered against prescription privileges. I found many of those with an opposing point of view sincere in their beliefs, although in some cases, hidden agendas were rather transparent. It is worth considering the principal arguments against prescription privileges, and why I was not convinced. I should also say, in passing, that the medical doctors all indicated their great respect for psychologists before proceeding to say why they should not be allowed to prescribe drugs. In at least some cases, the respect appeared to be sincere!

## Rebuttals to arguments against prescription privileges

*Training.* First, some physicians argued that psychologists are not properly trained to prescribe drugs. Certainly many, and probably most of them, are not. No one is suggesting, however, that psychologists be given prescription privileges without their having the requisite training and supervised experience for doing so. Thus, this argument is, to a large extent, a straw person. I view this kind of training as likely to be largely, if not exclusively, postdoctoral. Because no one is suggesting that untrained people prescribe drugs, this argument is not persuasive.

*Understanding of the medical model.* Second, physicians argued that psychologists are not trained in the medical model and hence are not in a position to prescribe drugs based on a medical model. This argument will strike many contemporary psychologists as curious. Today, many psychologists are trained in a biopsychosocial model, which we view as superior to the medical model. Indeed, the medical model is, at best, a special case of the biopsychosocial model currently being used in psychological practice. It often tends to be oriented toward treating illnesses rather than toward promoting wellness. I believe that the model under which psychologists are trained is actually more appropriate for prescribing drugs than is the narrower, exclusively medical model.

*Some apparently psychological problems are not really psychological.* Third, some of the medical doctors who testified pointed out that certain apparently psychological problems are caused by medical problems, which psychologists would be in a position neither to treat nor even to recognize. Therefore, it would be dangerous to give prescription privileges to psychologists. Of course, the medical doctors are right on the first score. But there is an error in the logic. The error is in assuming that anyone is competent to treat all possible illnesses. In fact, no one is competent to treat all possible illnesses. Medical doctors often need to make referrals, just as psychologists do. It always makes sense for any person seeking psychological help to have a complete physical examination, especially if there is even the remote possibility that a psychological condition may be connected to a physical one. Just as medical doctors can and often do make referrals to psychologists, similarly, psychologists can and often do make referrals to medical doctors. All professionals have to work together to offer the best treatment possible, and a team approach may be appropriate in special cases. But a team approach may be appropriate, regardless of the professional care-giver the person in need originally approaches.

*Amount of education for and experience in treating those in need.* Fourth, some of the medical doctors seemed to be under the impression that they had more education for and experience in treating people in need than did psychologists. This impression simply is false. Testimony revealed the amount of education and experience to be quite comparable, on average. What differs is the kind of training and the kind of experience. But of course, this difference would apply even within the medical profession. Those who plan to specialize in anesthesiology will have different experiences from those who plan to specialize in psychiatry.

*The unspoken agenda item.* Fifth, there was one unspoken agenda item that loomed large in the testimony of some of the medical doctors. Right now, medical doctors have prescription privileges to themselves. Granting such privileges to psychologists might and probably would cut into their incomes. And physicians, like psychologists, have been adversely affected by managed care. They, too, are for the most part uninterested in plans that augur even worse for their incomes than have managed-care plans. Their concerns are understandable. At the same time, they might find that increased collaborations with psychologists also would provide new sources of income. Often, doing what is best for everyone is not only wise, but in the long run, is optimally rewarding for everyone.

To summarize, I believe that the preponderance of considerations leads to the conclusion that psychologists ought to have the option of receiving advanced training that will lead to prescription privileges for them in their practices. Ultimately, everyone would benefit.

# 9

# Psychologists Should Not Be Licensed to Prescribe Psychiatric Drugs

## Stephen Barrett

*Stephen Barrett is a retired psychiatrist. He is also the vice president of the National Council Against Health Fraud, a scientific adviser to the American Council on Science and Health, and a fellow of the Committee for the Scientific Investigation of Claims of the Paranormal.*

Legislation that would allow psychologists to prescribe psychiatric drugs to their patients should not be passed. Even with the additional training such licensing would require, psychologists will not be adequately prepared to safely prescribe drugs. Psychiatrists complete four years of medical training, learning biochemistry, pharmacology, and diagnosis. In addition, they spend at least three years in postgraduate training, prescribing drugs under supervision to hundreds of patients. Clearly, unless psychologists go back to medical school, they will lack such qualifications to properly prescribe drugs and risk not fully understanding how drugs interact with each other, possible dangerous side effects, and what to do if such side effects develop. Allowing psychologists prescription privileges puts patients' health and safety at risk. In addition, psychologists who elect to prescribe medications will face serious legal risks. Should even a few malpractice suits against psychologists prescribing drugs be successful, their insurance coverage would become prohibitively expensive or no longer be offered.

The American Psychological Association and at least 30 state psychological associations are seeking passage of state laws that would enable psychologists to prescribe psychiatric medications to their patients. Psychologists have also stepped up efforts to establish psychopharmacology training programs.

In March 2002, New Mexico became the first state to authorize psychologist prescribing. Its new law (*HB 170*) enables psychologists to ac-

quire a two-year license to prescribe under physician supervision by:
- Completing at least 450 hours of coursework that includes psychopharmacology, neuroanatomy, neurophysiology, clinical pharmacology, pharmacology, pathophysiology, pharmacotherapeutics, pharmacoepidemiology, and physical and laboratory assessments.
- Completing a 400 hour/100 patient practicum under physician supervision.
- Passing a national certification examination.

Then, if the supervisor approves and the psychologist's prescribing records pass an independent peer review, the psychologist can apply to prescribe independently. To maintain prescribing ability, the psychologist must carry malpractice insurance, complete 20 hours of continuing education annually, and collaborate with the patient's primary physician. The new law also enables prescribing psychologists to order relevant laboratory tests.

## Opposition to licensing

The key question is whether training of this type will enable psychologists to prescribe safely and effectively for their patients. The American Medical Association, the American Psychiatric Association, the American Academy of Child and Adolescent Psychiatry, and many individual psychologists believe that the answer is no. I agree with this position.

---

*"Psychologists simply do not have the background or experience to safely and effectively use powerful medications in the treatment of mental illnesses."*

---

The American Psychiatric Association has labeled New Mexico's new law "the result of a cynical, economically-motivated effort by some elements of organized psychology to achieve legislated prescriptive authority without benefit of medical education and training." In a strongly worded statement, APA president Richard K. Harding, M.D., said:

> We believe that the legislature and the governor in New Mexico have placed patient health and safety at risk. . . . By virtue of their training and education, psychologists simply do not have the background or experience to safely and effectively use powerful medications in the treatment of mental illnesses. Psychologists have always had a clear path to prescribing privileges: medical school. No psychology-designed and administered crash course in drug prescribing can substitute for the comprehensive knowledge and skills physicians achieve through medical education and rigorous clinical experience. . . .

> Over the past decade, 14 state legislatures have rejected psychology prescribing legislation after objectively considering the scientific data and the public health risks of placing potent medications for treatment of mental illness in the hands

of people with no medical education or residency training. We hope that they will continue to do so in the future.

The Society for the Science of Clinical Psychology (SSCP), a section of the American Psychological Association, is also opposed to psychologist prescribing. Its members are concerned not only that patients will be improperly treated, but also that psychologists will face serious legal risks. In July 2001, SSCP members voted 98-6 to adopt a position statement which states (in part):

- No satisfactory precedents exist, either for designing suitable training programs or for predicting psychologists' performance as prescribers.
- Few existing psychologists would be able to complete any acceptable training program.
- Graduate education in basic psychological science and psychosocial treatments would be severely diminished and distorted unless most or all biomedical coursework were at the postdoctoral level.
- Malpractice premiums would go up for those who elect to prescribe, and possibly for all licensed psychologists, whether they prescribe or not.
- Should even a few malpractice suits against prescribing psychologists based on claims of inadequate medical training be successful, insurance coverage would become prohibitively expensive or disappear altogether.
- Psychologists would be exposed to patients' demands for "pill fixes" and the blandishments of the pharmaceutical industry, just as psychiatric and other medical professionals already are.

## Inherent risks

I oppose psychologist prescribing because I don't see how it is possible for a one-year course to adequately prepare nonphysicians to prescribe psychiatric drugs. To properly prescribe drugs, it is necessary to know when they should be prescribed, when they should not be prescribed, how they might interact with other drugs, what side effects might occur, and what to do when adverse effects do occur. If new symptoms occur, it is important to know whether they are related to taking a drug or represent a new problem that requires medical care.

Psychiatrists undergo four years of medical school during which they learn biochemistry, pharmacology, and diagnosis. Then they have at least three years of full-time postgraduate psychiatric training during which they typically prescribe drugs (under supervision) for hundreds of patients. And once in practice, the vast majority learn more by reading journals, talking with colleagues, and attending continuing education courses. I don't see how a part-time one-year course can provide anything comparable for psychologists.

# 10

# Talk Therapy
# Helps Heal Depression

## Milton Hammerly

*Milton Hammerly is a family physician and the medical director of complementary and alternative medicine for the Catholic Health Initiatives' Centura Health facilities nationwide.*

People suffering from depression can benefit from various forms of talk therapy because it gives them the chance to express their feelings and to change behaviors and thoughts that create depression. Several types of psychotherapy are particularly effective in treating depression. Cognitive therapy focuses on helping people to identify and change patterns of negative thinking that contribute to depression. Behavioral therapists, on the other hand, guide people to change self-destructive behaviors and take new actions to improve their lives. Group therapists also can help people to heal depression by providing a safe place where group members can share feelings and find support in difficult times.

No one is born depressed. Gaze into the eyes of a healthy infant and you'll see an innocent mix of excitement and inner peace. Look into the eyes of a seriously depressed adult and you may glimpse unspeakable despair, or worse, the eerie absence of any real feeling. Somewhere along the line, something changed.

We know from our growing understanding of the complex interplay of brain biochemistry and hormonal activity that too much or too little of this neurotransmitter or that hormone—or the right amounts made available at the wrong time—can have profound effects on our thoughts, emotions, and mood. Sometimes we seem to be transformed into someone we scarcely recognize.

But this body-mind connection is a two-way street. Not only do neurotransmitters and hormones affect how we think and feel, our thoughts and feelings can dramatically alter hormone levels and neurotransmitter activity in the brain. In other words, not only can our brains change our minds; *we can use our minds to change our brains.*

That's the idea behind many forms of talk therapy; to reprogram our brains for healthier, more productive functioning. Psychotherapy, once thought to work because it helped release unresolved conflicts buried deep in the unconscious, is now believed to be effective because, over time, it may literally restructure the biochemistry of depression in the brain.

Depression is the quintessential mind-body disease. You can attack depression from the "body" side with various herbs, antidepressants, phototherapy, biofeedback, and dozens of other treatments. Or you can approach it from the "mind" side with various stress reduction techniques and talk therapies. When depression arises from a treatable physical/biochemical condition, clearly a "body" approach is called for. When there seems to be no serious underlying physical disorder and when depression is mild to moderate, a "mind-centered" approach may be appropriate. Depending on the type and degree of the depression many people find a *combination* of body and mind therapies to be the most powerful treatment for the relief and prevention of depressive disorders.

The road to effective treatment begins with an accurate diagnosis—not only to "type" your depression, but to assess your overall physical health. Once you have a clear picture of your mental and physical status, you may wish to consider various talk therapy options.

## What is talk therapy?

The simplest form of talk therapy is simply talking—discussing problems or feelings, past or present, with a close friend, a family member, a member of the clergy, a teacher, a neighbor, or even a complete stranger you meet on a train. The mere act of expressing yourself, telling your story, or admitting vulnerability can be very therapeutic, regardless of who's listening. That's why even talking into a tape recorder or writing letters you may never actually send can be a step on the path to healing.

On the other hand, getting stuck in a constant litany of complaints—how horrible your life is, how someone wronged you, how you can never do anything right, how no one understands you—can actually reinforce and perpetuate your problems.

Serious depression deserves professional help. In professional talk therapy, a psychologist, psychiatrist, social worker, or trained counselor listens to your thoughts and feelings, identifies issues related to your mental and emotional state, and helps you think more clearly about how you can create a more satisfying life.

For moderate to severe depression, a combination of psychotherapy and antidepressants often leads to the best outcomes. Antidepressants can help you stay focused so you get more out of psychotherapy, and psychotherapy can provide emotional support until antidepressant treatments begin to work—which can take up to six weeks or longer.

## Who benefits from talk therapy?

Say the word "therapy" and many people still imagine a self-centered patient lying on an expensive couch, droning on about his or her problems, while a bearded doctor silently takes notes. That's hardly the case these days. Psychotherapy today is really an extended conversation between a client and an attentive mental health professional. You describe your problems, symptoms, experiences, past and present thoughts, emotions, behaviors, and relationships, and your therapist offers insight and feedback. She can't solve your problems, but she can help you find sensible solutions that are right for you.

Psychotherapy can help undo some of the damage depression has inflicted on your self-esteem. You may feel dull and uninteresting, almost invisible. If you have bipolar disorder, you may feel unstable, unreliable, and out of control as you fluctuate between episodes of depression and mania. You may even begin to believe your disease defines who you are. Therapy can help turn your life around by changing the behaviors or thought patterns that created or maintained your depression, and by preventing another bout of depression. It can help you start enjoying life again.

Your primary-care physician may recommend therapy as the main treatment if you have mild-to-moderate depression that's lasted only a few weeks and hasn't occurred before. He may also suggest combining therapy with exercise, diet modifications, or alternative treatments such as the herb St. John's wort for a more natural approach to managing your depression.

Many people prefer therapy because they'd rather not take antidepressants and risk unpleasant side effects. On the other hand, some people are dead-set against therapy. They see it as embarrassing or even shameful and feel that taking a medication is more "socially acceptable." They erroneously believe that therapy is for "weak" people, and that strong people can handle their own problems and pull themselves together.

---

*Psychotherapy . . . may literally restructure the biochemistry of depression in the brain.*

---

If you happen to fall into this category, here are some facts to consider. Years of research studies have proven that therapy is enormously valuable in helping depressed patients. In fact, a 1998 study in the *Journal of Consulting and Clinical Psychology* suggests that therapy may be just as good as antidepressants for certain people. Two groups with major depression were followed for eight months. Those receiving only psychotherapy improved just as significantly as those receiving only antidepressants. In a less severely depressed group, people getting psychotherapy didn't improve as quickly as those on antidepressants, but after four months of treatment, both groups showed similar improvement.

Several types of psychotherapy are effective for treating depression. How you relate to your therapist is generally more important than the type of therapy used. Experienced therapists almost always use a combination of approaches, custom-fitting the treatment to the client's style and needs.

Because depression has many potential emotional and mental causes—such as abusive relationships, past conflicts, repressed emotions, pessimistic thinking, negative behaviors, or major losses—your therapist must consider your personal situation before deciding on a particular treatment approach. How you respond to one type of therapy over another depends on your personal issues, your problem-solving style, your level of commitment to feeling better, and the strength of your personal support systems. The following information will help you understand the various types of psychotherapy and choose a therapist who's right for you.

## Short-term therapies

Opponents of long-term psychotherapy argue that it can go on for years without any end in sight and with no way for the patient to know when he's "cured." Actually, long-term therapies such as Freudian psychoanalysis have largely been replaced by shorter-term therapies, which are more effective, more efficient, and less expensive. A National Institute of Mental Health (NIMH) study showed that 55 percent of mild-to-moderately depressed people felt significantly better after only 16 weeks of psychotherapy.

---

*Many people prefer therapy because they'd rather not take antidepressants and risk unpleasant side effects.*

---

Managed care is another reason for the surge in short-term therapy. Managed care plans and HMOs limit the number of therapy visits per year, based on the *DSM* [*Diagnostic and Statistical Manual of Mental Disorders*] diagnosis. But this doesn't necessarily mean that patients are getting shortchanged. Therapists are compelled to be more efficient and develop new, effective brief-therapy programs. When problems do arise, it may be due to an inadequate number of visits or it may be that therapists are forced to fit all patients into specific therapeutic models, even when they don't conform.

Short-term therapy typically lasts between five to 20 sessions, emphasizes present rather than past problems, and sets concrete, attainable goals that require the client and therapist to actively work together. Cognitive and behavioral therapy are especially effective for the treatment of depression.

## Cognitive therapy

Cognitive therapy—also called cognitive restructuring—helps people identify and consciously change patterns of negative thinking that lead to or maintain depression. Developed in the 1970s by psychiatrist Aaron T. Beck of the University of Pennsylvania, the approach was designed specifically to treat depression. While [the nineteenth-century Austrian founder of psychoanalysis] Sigmund Freud suggested that how we feel influences what we think, Beck postulated that what we think determines how we feel. Both theories are valid.

When we engage in negative thinking—what Beck calls "cognitive distortions"—we tend to blow minor incidents out of proportion until they seem like catastrophes. If you're already depressed, this is like running your own black cloud machine.

Psychiatrist David Burns, Beck's colleague and the author of *Feeling*

*Good: The New Mood Therapy*, looks for ten types of negative thinking, including these:

> *All-or-nothing thinking:* Perfectionism; seeing everything in terms of black and white. If you make a mistake at work, you're a failure. If someone hurts you, they're all bad.

> *Labeling:* All-or-nothing thinking taken one step further. If you lock yourself out of the house, you didn't just make a mistake, you're an idiot.

> *Mental filtering:* Dwelling on the negative aspects of a situation, while ignoring the positive. If you give a speech and one person in the back row says he had trouble hearing you, you obsess over this one complaint instead of enjoying all the compliments you receive.

> *"Should" and "shouldn't" statements:* If you get a B on a test, you chastise yourself, thinking "I should've gotten an A."

Such self-defeating thinking makes even small sucesses a struggle. Your therapist will help you restructure these destructive thought patterns into positive, realistic statements so you can say to yourself, "I made a mistake, but I learned from it. Next time I'll do better."

The cognitive therapist uses five basic techniques to turn your thinking around:

- Recognizing negative thoughts that may automatically enter your consciousness when you're feeling your worst
- Disputing negative thoughts by focusing on contrary evidence
- Applying different explanations to dispute negative thoughts
- Controlling your thoughts and avoiding rumination
- Replacing negative thoughts with more empowering positive thoughts and beliefs

Your therapist will help you rehearse new, positive thought patterns to replace habitual, negative thinking. One way she does this is by having you keep a diary of your negative thoughts and the incidents that prompted them. For example, your assignment may be to write five pages in a week. Just the act of writing down your negative thoughts is therapeutic. Putting your thoughts on paper makes it easier to see that they're irrational. Saying them aloud helps, too. As you progress in therapy, your therapist may have you go back and rewrite your negative thoughts as more positive statements or take some concrete actions.

In another tactic called "cognitive rehearsal," you imagine a difficult situation and then plan a step-by-step approach to the problem. Your therapist helps you obliterate negative "I can't" thoughts and replace them with positive "I can" ones.

Cognitive therapy takes effort. Long-standing thought patterns are hard to break. On the other hand, the steps to recovery—mainly being aware of your negative emotions and what triggers them and then making substitutions—seem too facile to some people. But simplicity is cognitive therapy's strong point. It's quick and easy once you understand how it works, and it's easy to apply in your real life.

## Behavioral therapy

Unlike cognitive therapy, which strives to change negative thoughts, behavioral therapy strives to change unproductive, self-destructive behavior. While other psychotherapies are geared toward increasing your awareness or helping you find the root causes of your problems, behavioral therapy helps you find the tools to actively change your life.

Behavioral therapy arose from laboratory experiments with animals that involved positive and negative reinforcement, conditioned reflexes, and other learning principles. Behavior therapy techniques are most effective in treating people with specific problem behaviors, such as eating disorders (anorexia or bulimia), alcoholism, drug abuse, smoking, anxiety, or procrastination—which often coexist with depression. However, this type of therapy is less effective than cognitive therapy for treating major depression, unless the depression involves a behavioral problem.

To change counterproductive or destructive behaviors, therapists give clients "assignments" to complete by the next session. These assignments take the form of behavior modification, systematic desensitization and exposure therapy, or assertiveness training.

- *Behavior modification* aims to break self-destructive behavior patterns by rewarding positive behavior. For example, if your problem is smoking, your therapist might ask you to buy yourself a gift if you go a week without a cigarette.
- *Systematic desensitization and exposure therapy* helps people with anxiety or phobias, which often accompany depression. If you are afraid to meet new people, for example, the therapist will ask you to gradually immerse yourself in various social situations—at first, encouraging you to go out only with people you know well, eventually working up to attending a party where you'll be introduced to strangers.
- *Assertiveness training* systematically trains you to clearly state your thoughts and feelings and stand your ground despite objections. Your "homework" might be to speak your mind when your husband says something that hurts or angers you, or to practice asking directly for something you want.

The strength of behavioral therapy is that it zeroes in on specific problems, offers concrete ways to change behavior, and provides skills that you can use after therapy is over. But the success of this short-term therapy is entirely dependent on how often and how consistently you apply the behavior modification techniques after you leave the session. . . .

## Group therapies

In the following therapy models, more than one person works with a therapist or group leader. These therapies emphasize the "unit" rather than the individual and can be very effective in treating certain types of depression.

*Family Therapy.* Instead of dealing with just one person, as in traditional psychotherapy, family therapy treats the family as a unit and aims to change the way members relate to each other. Depression is considered an expression of not merely one person but of a dysfunctional family. This type of therapy may be helpful in treating depression in instances where a person's depression is caused by a serious family problem (for example, marital discord or a partner's alcoholism) or where a person's depression jeopardizes family relationships.

Family therapy focuses on breaking destructive cycles of behavior, improving communication among family members, and finding more effective ways of coping with stressful family situations. It also explores ways family members can better support each other and work toward common goals, while maintaining a sense of individual independence. Although one person's depression may be the impetus for therapy, other family members should be prepared to examine their lives and behaviors, too.

---

*Therapy is enormously valuable in helping depressed patients.*

---

Some therapists include children as young as four years old in family therapy sessions; others prefer to wait until children are at least nine or ten. Anyone living in your home may take part, including elderly parents or nonrelatives who play important roles in your family life.

Models of family therapy range from a psychoanalytic approach that examines unconscious conflicts to a behavioral approach directed toward changing family behavior patterns through positive and negative reinforcement. The most recent family therapy models were developed by Nathan Ackerman (considered the father of family therapy), Jay Haley, Virginia Satir, and others.

Ackerman was the first to suggest that therapists should actively participate and shake things up by moving the family out of predictable patterns of behavior and responding. Several interactive techniques are used, such as role reversal, in which individuals switch roles with other family members and act out a typical problem situation. Role reversal can teach communication and problem-solving skills, help people deal better with conflict, and enhance empathy.

Variations on family therapy include "network family therapy," where friends, neighbors, or even employers are involved in sessions, and "multiple family therapy," where several families meet as a group.

The length of family therapy varies. Brief therapy may take place in three to 10 sessions. In longer-term therapy, patients usually see a therapist once a week for six to eight weeks, then check back every month or two for several months. Sessions usually last an hour and a half. This therapy won't be effective unless all family members are open and cooperative. Depressed people may also require individual therapy to work on other, specific issues. . . .

## Guidelines for group therapy

Although it's a popular form of psychotherapy, group therapy isn't recommended for a severely depressed person whose low self-esteem and low energy level prevent him from actively participating in conversation. However, once antidepressants or individual therapy begin to relieve depression, a sympathetic group where you can openly share your feelings can be a very effective way to gain a greater acceptance of yourself, learn more effective ways to cope, and find support in difficult times.

Group therapy often consists of six to 10 people meeting weekly for an hour and a half. It may continue for a predetermined amount of time, go on indefinitely, or break up when members lose interest. Participants are chosen by the therapist, and although they must all have the same goal for the group to work, they don't necessarily need to have the same problems. Mixed groups (different ages, sexes, and problems) more closely reflect the real world. Homogeneous groups (alcoholics, depressed people, couples) make it easier to share experiences.

The therapist sets the ground rules, guides discussions, and resolves conflicts. Some therapists remain neutral, while others actively promote group interaction. Members are encouraged to be frank and spontaneous. With time, they see how their patterns of interacting with others might help or hurt them in relationships outside the group.

Group therapy is especially helpful for depressed people who have concurrent problems like substance abuse or eating disorders. It can also be much less expensive than individual therapy, and sessions last twice as long. The downside is that depressed people can't focus on their own problems for the entire session (although each member is given some time to talk). Therefore, many people in group therapy choose to see an individual therapist concurrently.

# 11

# Electroconvulsive Therapy Is an Effective Treatment

## Max Fink

*Max Fink is an emeritus professor of psychiatry and neurology at State University of New York at Stony Brook and a professor of psychiatry at Albert Einstein College of Medicine. He is also the author of* Electroshock: Restoring the Mind.

Studies have shown electroshock treatment, now known as electroconvulsive therapy, to be an effective treatment for depression, mania, delusional states, and catatonia in adolescents and adults, including the elderly. However, the public view of the treatment has been extremely negative, due in part to films such as the 1975 classic *One Flew over the Cuckoo's Nest,* in which the protagonist is forced to undergo both electroshock treatment and a lobotomy. In addition, the use of psychotropic drugs developed in the 1950s and 1960s began to displace electroshock because they were much less expensive and had fewer immediate risks. Nonetheless, a few psychiatrists continued to use electroshock and found that their patients benefited. Scientists and manufacturers also improved the treatment devices and greatly reduced any risks of long-term cognitive damage. Although scientists still do not understand exactly why electroshock has the ability to heal people, it clearly is effective in relieving some mental disorders. More research is needed to find out its mechanism of healing. Further, the public needs to be educated to understand electroshock's benefits and to accept its use for the mentally ill who have not benefited from other therapies.

Electroconvulsive therapy, once vilified, is slowly receiving greater interest and use in the treatment of mental illness.

Scene: The winter of 1934, inside a state hospital for the mentally ill at Lipotmezo, Hungary.

Zoltan, a 30-year-old Budapest laborer, lay rigidly in a bed, staring into the distance. Except for his slow and regular breathing, he appeared lifeless. He had hardly spoken or cared for himself in more than four years. His mental condition of catatonic schizophrenia was considered hopeless. No remedy was available and none was sought; the doctors believed the illness to be an immutable genetic fault. At 10:30 on the morning of January 24, 1934, the Hungarian neuropsychiatrist Ladislas Meduna approached Zoltan's bed to inject an oily extract of camphor into his right buttock. Zoltan's heart soon raced, sweat rose on his brow, and he became increasingly fearful. After 45 minutes, his eyes suddenly closed, his jaw clenched, his breathing stopped, and he lost consciousness. With a deep, noisy sigh, his arms and legs extended, he convulsed, and his bed thumped rhythmically, attendants caught him just before he rolled to the floor. His skin became ashen, and he wet the bed. After 60 seconds, as suddenly as the spasm started, it ended. His eyes opened, and a pink color slowly returned to his cheeks. He continued to stare and was as speechless as before. He had survived an intentionally induced grand mal epileptic fit.

Without any guideline as to how often seizures should be induced, Meduna adopted the schedule used in the popular malarialfever treatment of neurosyphilis. He injected camphor at three- to four-day intervals, and two days after the fifth seizure, Zoltan awakened, looked about, got out of bed, asked where he was and requested breakfast. He did not believe that he had been in the hospital for four years, and he knew nothing of the intervening history. Later that day, he again relapsed into stupor. After each of the next induced seizures, Zoltan remained alert and interested for longer and longer periods, until after the eighth injection he left the hospital to return to his home and to work. His mental condition of four years was fully relieved. Five years later, when Meduna left Europe for the United States, Zoltan was still well and working at his job.

## Electroshock is making a comeback

This dramatic account of Zoltan's recovery from schizophrenia describes the first use of the technique that evolved into electroshock, also now called electroconvulsive therapy, or simply ECT. As the modern name suggests, the method now involves the use of electrical currents to induce grand mal seizures as a treatment for mental illness. Electroshock is applied to about 100,000 patients each year in the U.S., a figure comparable to the number of appendectomies or hernial surgeries performed. Its efficacy and safety has been recognized by the U.S. Surgeon General in his Report on Mental Health, which was released in December 1999. Clinical trials on disorders other than schizophrenia have found ECT to be effective in depression, mania, delusional states and catatonia—in the elderly and in adolescents as well as adults—and it can be safely applied to patients with severe physical illnesses. Despite electroshock's successes, it is severely restricted by legislation in several states and continues to have an undeservedly poor image in the public mind. Fortunately, there is a growing trend to restore ECT to a reasoned place in psychiatric practice. Here I provide a brief review of the history and present state of electroconvulsive therapy, and some thoughts on its mechanism of action.

## The evolution of ECT

Shortly after his success with Zoltan, Meduna treated five other schizophrenic patients—each of whom recovered. Published reports of Meduna's successes galvanized clinicians throughout the world. The notion that dementia praecox (as schizophrenia was then called) could be relieved at all was remarkable to many who believed that the disease was relentlessly progressive and hopeless. Nowadays it is difficult for us to appreciate how revolutionary such an achievement appeared.

---

*Electroshock is applied to about 100,000 patients each year in the U.S.*

---

Although the camphor-based treatment was successful, it was not without its drawbacks: The injections were painful, and the seizure developed after an agonizing and frightening delay of many minutes. Another chemical, Metrazol, induced a fit quickly when injected intravenously. Within a minute, the patient's thoughts raced, his heart beat rapidly, terror filled the mind, and consciousness was lost. After a few minutes of seizing, the patient slowly reawakened, his muscles, back and head ached, and often his tongue and lips were bleeding. Memory of recent events was erased. Despite the risks and terrors, and the need for repeated frequent injections to achieve a benefit, Metrazol-seizure therapy was widely adopted. Its success changed public and professional attitudes toward mental illness from one of hopeless resignation to optimism that relief was possible.

Ways were sought to reduce the risks of chemically induced seizures. In 1938, the Italians Ugo Cerletti and Luigi Bini induced seizures using electricity applied through electrodes placed on both temples. The seizure was immediate and just as effective as those induced by intravenous chemicals, and the new technique avoided the initial fearfulness and panic. The technique was so easy that within a few years electroconvulsive therapy became the dominant treatment of the severely mentally ill.

The risks persisted, however. The treatments were administered without anesthesia and often resulted in fractures and in severe memory loss. Occasionally, patients suffered a second seizure after leaving the treatment room. The treatments were unpleasant; patients often had to be coaxed, and occasionally forced, to treatment.

Fears of this experience, especially the effects on memory and recall, limited its use. Impaired breathing and the high electrical energies commonly used in the early decades severely impaired the brain's functions. Patients could not recall events during the illness and during the period of treatment. Many lost memories of their early life and were left with feelings of strangeness—that they were living dreams in which much that should be familiar was not. . . .

## Drugs, politics, and electroshock therapy

The development of psychotropic medicines in the 1950s and 1960s spelled the beginning of a dark period in electroshock's history. The drugs—Thorazine for psychosis, Tofranil for depression, Miltown for anxiety and lithium for mania—ushered in the present era of psychopharmacology. The medicines were easy to administer, carried few immediate risks and were much less expensive. ECT was confined to the dustbin of history.

The political climate in the 1960s and 1970s did little to foster the use of ECT. The new drugs had been lauded for doing away with the large, impersonal state mental hospitals, and the phaseout of the nation's mental-hospital system was in full swing. Their professional staffs had discarded ECT, and it was virtually impossible to re-establish the physical facilities for the treatments or find the trained personnel to carry them out. The nation had been through the political and social upheaval of the Vietnam conflict; the actions of any authority, governmental or medical, were challenged. Legislators were deluged with calls to outlaw what were perceived as coercive psychiatric treatments—psychotropic medicines, electroshock and lobotomy. The California legislature heeded this call in 1973 and banned the use of electroshock and lobotomy. The law was struck down by the courts as an improper incursion into medical practice, but a judicially acceptable bill regulating the treatments became law the next year. It severely inhibits the practice of ECT in that state.

Many public events also cast a pall over the use of electroshock. After a successful senate career, the 1972 vice presidential candidate Thomas Eagleton was forced from the Democratic ticket when the press trumpeted that he had received this treatment for depression. In the widely hailed 1975 film *One Flew Over the Cuckoo's Nest*, the protagonist suffers both electroshock and lobotomy at the hands of unbridled caretakers. Viewers leave the theater with sympathy for the patients and hostility to the caretakers. In popular books the psychiatrist Thomas Szasz castigated psychiatrists as agents of the state who coerced the mentally ill into forced and unwelcome hospital care. He especially criticized the use of electroshock. His student, Peter Breggin, canvassed Congress to outlaw the physical treatments of the mentally ill, espousing love and talk therapy as effective agents of change. Ron Hubbard, as part of the mission of his Church of Scientology, unleashed a national attack on psychiatry, which is active today in energizing state legislatures to proscribe psychiatric treatments.

## Improved electroshock methods benefit patients

Despite a national climate of outrage and vilification, a few psychiatrists continued to use ECT for patients who had failed treatment with medicines and found that their patients benefited. Reports of such success encouraged manufacturers to improve the treatment devices; scientists again sought ways to improve the practice and reduce the risks; and commissions began to write manuals for proper treatment. By the 1980s, the federal government supported studies of how best to decrease the effects on cognition and memory. Technical improvements emerged quickly, so much so that in its present use ECT is considered as safe as psychotropic medicines. Indeed, for the elderly, for those weakened by systemic diseases and for pregnant women with severe mental illnesses, ECT is safer than the alternative treatments.

There is an uneven distribution of facilities providing the treatment. Most university hospitals treat about 5 to 10 percent of their mentally ill adult patients with ECT, whereas the treatment rates at state, federal and Veterans Administration hospitals are much lower because few have the facilities. Community and private hospitals vary widely in their ability to offer the treatment. This results in a haphazard application of ECT.

Legal proscriptions inhibit its proper use. In California, Texas and Tennessee, electroshock is interdicted in children and young adolescents. The legislatures in Arizona, Vermont and Texas have been considering restrictive legislation. In some states, patients may only be treated with electroshock after physicians and independent consultants certify that all other methods of treatment have been tried and failed, an impossible standard to satisfy, consigning the mentally ill to long periods of illness before an effective treatment is given. At times, the treatment is offered too late, the patients having died by suicide or inanition while awaiting court approval for treatment.

## How does ECT work?

Why are seizures, which are dangerous and damaging when they occur spontaneously, beneficial when induced experimentally? For the moment scientists have no answer to this question—we simply don't understand how ECT has the restorative capacity that it does. For that matter, no hypothesis for the mode of action of any psychiatric treatment—be it electroshock, psychotropic medicines or the "talk" psychotherapies—is satisfactory.

Explanations for the mechanism of ECT tend to be similar to those used to explain the therapeutic actions of the psychoactive drugs. Most commonly the explanations are focused on the messenger molecules, or neurotransmitters, that pass from one neuron to another. Among the more notable of these molecules are dopamine, serotonin, norepinephrine and gamma-amino-butyric acid (GABA)—neurotransmitters that are typically central to biologically based theories of mental illness. Each of these molecules binds to specific receptors on neuronal-cell surfaces and in turn modifies the activity of these neurons. Psychotropic medicines alter the concentrations of these neurotransmitters and so modify the activity of neurons in certain parts of the brain, most notably those areas believed to play important roles in mental disorders. How the activity of these neurons translates into thoughts and feelings is the big question now facing neuroscientists.

*[Electroshock therapy] is considered as safe as psychotropic medicines.*

There is a fundamental difficulty with extending the neurotransmitter—based hypotheses to the mechanism of electroshock, however—one that goes beyond the question of how these messenger molecules play a role in the brain. Experiments involving seizures induced in animals and people reveal that so many neurotransmitters are released in what appears to be a random way that it is difficult to construct a cogent theory.

Another theory of electroshock's mechanism involves the observation that the threshold needed to induce a seizure rises during the course of a successful series of treatments. After anesthesia, it is possible to stimulate the brain with different dosages of electric current. By selecting currents that are too low to elicit a seizure and repeating this procedure with incremental energies, a seizure threshold can be defined as that amount of energy that is sufficient to elicit an effective grand mal seizure. If the seizure threshold is defined in subsequent treatments, we observe a gradual rise in seizure threshold. If the energies are kept constant, the duration of the elicited seizure falls. In successful courses of treatment, seizure thresholds are known to rise. The rise in seizure threshold varies with the rise in cerebral blood flow, slowing of EEG [electroencephalograph] frequencies and the antidepressant effects of electroshock.

---

*[Electroshock therapy] is very broadly effective in relieving mental disorders.*

---

Some authors conclude that the antidepressant efficacy of electroshock is related to the anticonvulsant activity of repeated seizures, as reflected in the rise in seizure threshold. The anticonvulsant theory is also encouraged by the efficacy of anticonvulsant medicines in relieving mania. However, the theory is weakened by the failure of antidepressant drugs to raise seizure thresholds and the inability of benzodiazepines (anxiolytics such as diazepam) and other anticonvulsant drugs to elicit clinical antidepressant activity.

Despite their weaknesses, theories based on neurotransmitters, their receptor molecules and the anticonvulsant activity of electroshock have the most support today.

## Treatment no longer has to cause memory loss

There is, however, an alternative hypothesis. We know a great deal about what we must do to achieve ECT's clinical benefits. Seizures induced by chemicals are just as effective as those induced by electricity, indicating that electricity is not essential to our explanation. Neither anesthesia nor the electric current alone nor a single seizure is effective. At one time, memory impairment was an explanation for electroshock's effects, but we now achieve clinical efficacy without memory impairment and conclude that memory loss is not in the therapeutic chain.

We also know that ECT is very broadly effective in relieving mental disorders. It relieves depressed and manic moods, thought disorders and the motor disorders of catatonia and parkinsonism with almost equivalent efficacy. The most effective forms of ECT are those that directly stimulate the structures in the middle of the brain, as evidenced by the path of the electric current. What can we make of these observations? Whatever the mechanism involved, it appears to affect a broad range of systems in the body. And the central parts of the brain seem to play a key role in modulating electroshock's benefits.

This train of thought leads us to the hypothalamus, a region deep in the brain that is known to be involved in the expression of emotions and that has a profound control over the rest of the body through its actions on the pituitary gland. The hypothalamus, the pituitary and the pineal glands in the brain produce peptides that circulate in the bloodstream and the cerebrospinal fluid, affecting other glands in the body (including the thyroid, parathyroid, adrenal, pancreas, ovaries and testes) and other parts of the brain.

The importance of the hypothalamus in mental illness is consistent with the observation that hormonal functions in the mentally ill are wildly disordered. In the severely depressed, the adrenal glands produce too much cortisol, whereas the hypothalamus is inhibited in the release of its hormones and the pituitary functions are chaotic. During a seizure, massive amounts of the brain's hormones are released into the cerebrospinal fluid and into the bloodstream. How could such a release relieve mental disorders?

Consider the following scenario. Each electroshock stimulus is focused on the hypothalamus, eliciting an immediate and large discharge of its hormones. In the ensuing cascade of hormonal effects, the pituitary gland discharges its products, and those, in turn, alter the discharge of cortisol from the adrenal glands. The first effects of the brainstem stimulations are transitory, but by the fourth or fifth stimulus, the normal feedback actions of the hormones of the hypothalamicpituitary-adrenal axis are again in place. Feeding and sleep become normal, and improvements in motor activity, mood, memory and thought follow quickly.

In treating the mentally ill, the improved endocrine functions persist after a course of treatment, and the patient remains well. At other times, the glands quickly revert to their abnormal activities, and the mental disorder is again evident. In such cases, continuation ECT is needed to sustain normal glandular functions and a normal mental state.

How the rush of hormones resets the endocrine balance is not known. I propose that the brain secretes a hormonelike substance that regulates mental functions. Unfortunately, research into such a relation is not encouraged by government agencies, which are wary of the public's apprehension toward electroshock. The pharmaceutical industry tends to follow a safe course of finding "me-too" substances that can be marketed, and academic leaders often perceive ECT research as academically incorrect. Nevertheless, the broad efficacy of electroshock warrants greater attention to its therapeutic mechanism and to a campaign of education that will encourage its use for the many mentally ill who are poorly served by other therapies.

# 12

# Electroconvulsive Therapy Must Be Stopped

## John Breeding

*John Breeding is a psychologist in private practice in Austin, Texas. He is also the director of Texans for Safe Education, a citizens group that opposes increasing prescriptions of psychiatric drugs to schoolchildren. In addition, he is the director of Wildest Colts Resources, a nonprofit organization that trains adults to help troubled young people.*

It is wrong to force people to undergo a treatment as risky and controversial as electroshock therapy, which causes brain damage, memory loss, and sometimes even death. Forced electroshock violates people's civil rights and freedom of thought and choice. Doctors who force this procedure on their patients justify the abuse by perpetuating two lies. First, they declare that people who are "mentally ill" are incompetent, irrational, and dangerous and that, therefore, the state has the right to decide what is best for them. Labeling people in this way allows psychiatrists to treat them as less than human and to deprive them of their right to refuse the application of high-voltage electricity to the brain. Second, psychiatrists justify the use of electroshock therapy by asserting that it is a helpful treatment. In fact, it is an extremely dangerous and damaging procedure that has no positive lasting effects. Electroshock also causes the victims to suffer emotionally for years afterward.

My name is John Breeding. I am a psychologist from Austin, Texas. I have worked with many people in distress over 20 years of practice, including a number of victims of electroshock. I have also spent considerable time studying the research and writing on electroshock. . . . I have also been on the advisory board of the World Association of Electroshock Survivors, an organization consisting of individuals who at one time received this so-called treatment and later organized to push for a ban on electroshock.

I am convinced that electroshock is dangerous, harmful, and unnecessary. Doctors who perpetrate this procedure on their patients are committing a gross violation of their sacred Hippocratic oath, to "First, do no harm." The infliction of electroshock on an unconsenting individual,

John Breeding, testimony before the New York State Assembly, May 18, 2001.

which this hearing is addressing today, is one of our planet's greatest evils.

I want to say a bit more about the World Association of Electroshock Survivors. This and other groups like it, such as the Committee for Truth in Psychiatry and the larger Support Coalition International, represent thousands of individuals who received electroshock. Please reflect for a moment on the fact that these recipients of a supposedly beneficial therapeutic treatment are now organizing to actively seek a ban protecting their fellow citizens from the procedure because they conclude it has caused them permanent, grave harm. Have you ever heard of such a thing? If this were a standard medical procedure, there would surely be a serious re-evaluation of that procedure and probably a complete moratorium until proper investigation was completed. And if there were any substance at all to the claims, the procedure would likely be outlawed. At the very least, there would be a rigorous informed consent procedure explaining all risks and benefits . . . and most importantly and most assuredly, absolutely no one would be forced to undergo such a controversial and risky treatment.

---

*I am convinced that electroshock is dangerous, harmful, and unnecessary.*

---

This all seems clear and straightforward enough when you look at physical medicine. But there are many significant differences between physical medicine and psychiatry, most important of which is that no one is forced into physical medical treatment. Even the right to die is honored. Only in psychiatry is it literally true that adult citizens are forced to take their so-called medicine, including, of course, the "medicine" we are discussing today, electroshock.

## What justifies forced treatment?

I have spent many hours trying to understand the rationale for forced electroshock, and achieving such understanding is extremely difficult. Here in New York, the Statue of Liberty stands as a beacon to the world reminding all that America is synonymous with liberty. Our Supreme Court clearly acknowledges that psychiatric incarceration is a massive curtailment of civil rights. Forced electroshock is even worse; not only physical liberty is deprived, but also freedom of thought and feeling and expression. And not only the freedom, but even the ability is permanently altered and lessened.

How is it justified? The best I can figure is that there are two fundamental lies that justify such a brutal and ruthless violation of human freedom. The first is this: People labeled "mentally ill" are incompetent, irrational and dangerous. Therefore, it is the responsibility of the state as parens patriae of these unfortunate souls to do what is best for them. So this justifies massive curtailment of liberty and forced application of high voltage electricity to the brain, against an individual's wishes and informed consent, in a country that claims to place highest value on liberty and freedom of choice.

This hearing [on forced electroshock by the New York Assembly] has come about at least in part because of the ongoing legal challenge to the determined effort of Pilgrim Psychiatric Center psychiatrists to electroshock Paul Henri Thomas again and again and again, already more than 40 [times]! Listen to the following words of Mr. Thomas now in light of the tragic notion that forced electroshock is a justifiable deprivation of his liberty and freedom of choice because he is an incompetent, mentally ill, child-like sick person, incapable of rational choices about his treatment. As you listen, remember that you are not sitting in the anointed cabinet of a totalitarian dictatorship or politburo. Let his words come to you in your positions as elected representatives of the people of New York in the United States of America, a democracy where the principle of liberty is meant to reign supreme.

## Testimony of an electroshock patient

The words of Paul Henri Thomas:

> The forced electroshock is horrible. It is horrible. This torture and traumatization is not for what I did wrong. I am being tortured because I devoted myself to helping people as much as possible.

> I am aware that to obtain progress for humanity we have to suffer and endure. We have to absorb these things. Other people ask me whether I think my life is miserable because I receive forced electroshock. No. The people doing this to me are miserable. I have my pride and self-respect.

> I am strong. But no human being is invincible.

> This is an arbitrary process of court hearings and submitting me to a "court order" of electroshock treatment.

> Do something, please! I need my freedom. I have all the rights of a respectable human being and all his duties.

It is virtually impossible to really hear this man and fail to realize that a great and tragic act of oppression has taken place in New York under the auspices of state sanctioned psychiatry.

## Psychiatry dehumanizes people

Is his case or his eloquence unique? Not in my direct experience with scores of electroshock survivors. Paul Henri Thomas, like many others, is not being shocked because it is best for his "mental illness" that has rendered him dangerously incompetent. The sad truth is that he is shocked because psychiatry is bereft of understanding and compassion. Viewing individuals as dangerous and incompetent allows psychiatrists to treat them as less than human and justifies taking away their freedom and dignity and right of choice, hallmarks of their humanity.

As I grapple with attempting to understand how this horror is justified, the second thing I come up with is that those who force electroshock on people must assert that it is a good thing to do, a benevolent, helpful act. It would be hard to justify forced pain and brain damage—that's called torture, the stuff of cruel human rights violations evident throughout history and even to this day. Psychiatrists once acknowledged that electroshock's "therapeutic" effect was a result of brain damage, but have necessarily become more image conscious today. Autopsies of several decades ago routinely verified the brain damage, but autopsies following electroshock-related deaths are not performed today. Think about it: since the natural electrical activity of the brain is in millivolts (thousandths of a volt), how could a surge of 150 volts or more directly into the brain not cause brain damage? It is a challenge for all of us to retain our common sense in the face of confusing psychiatric rhetoric. The truth is pretty simple:

## The dangers of electroshock

Electroshock always causes brain damage. The question is only how much.

Electroshock always causes memory loss. The question is only how much.

Electroshock causes death. Published studies suggest the electroshock death rate is about 1 in 1000. Mortality for the elderly is much greater, about 1 in 200.

Did you know that we mostly shock our elderly? I am always at a loss to explain how psychiatric rhetoric can so cloud our basic judgement, compassion and respect for our elders that we assault them in their declining years with brain damaging electroshock and call it medical treatment. One 82-year-old woman, Lucille Austwick, was being threatened with forced electroshock, and she said, "Bull! Ridiculous!" Her friends went to court against the psychiatrists and saved her; unfortunately, many more are not saved. Elders are the most frequent victims, even though they are also at greatest risk of suffering grievous harm from electroshock.

---

*How could a surge of 150 volts or more directly into the brain not cause brain damage?*

---

The list of effects goes on and on, and it is an ugly picture. My own specialty is in the emotional area. There is no time for me to describe this here, but I want you to at least know that terror and shame are the regular effects of electroshock, especially forced electroshock. A woman I know, 74-year-old Mimi Greenberg of Austin, Texas, received forced electroshock. Afterwards, she was so frightened of all doctors that she dangerously neglected the real medical help she needed for many years. She shared with me that a significant part of her healing from this trauma was when she read a book of remembrances of holocaust survivors. She told me that these descriptions finally put words to the anguish she still felt from her experience with electroshock. Forced electroshock is not medicine; it is cruel torture.

Even when they acknowledge the real damage done by electroshock, its defenders still might attempt to justify it by saying the benefit is worth the dangers. Psychiatry says it works. Psychologist Harold Sackeim, of the

New York State Psychiatric Institute, keeps recommending it, even though he has just published an article which, when you get past all the verbiage, shows that virtually all of the patients had relapse within six months of receiving electroshock. Not only is electroshock dangerous and harmful. Not only is there no valid explanation for its effects other than brain damage. But also it simply has no positive lasting effects.

The plain truth is that there is no rational justification for forced electroshock. I appreciate your investigation today, and I urge you to pursue legislation ending the cruel practice of forced electroshock, and restoring the fundamental American rights of free choice inherent in authentic informed consent.

# 13

# Involuntary Treatment of the Mentally Ill Is Sometimes Necessary

### Rich Lowry

*Rich Lowry is the editor of the* National Review *magazine.*

In the past few decades numerous state psychiatric hospitals have closed, leaving many severely mentally ill people with grossly inadequate care. Most of these untreated people end up homeless or in prison, posing threats both to themselves and to their communities. These people are too sick to recognize that they need mental health treatment. Therefore, they need to receive involuntary treatment so that they have a chance to recover and escape their misery.

I encounter the mentally ill every day. I step over them on the sidewalks, I ignore their rantings, I look the other way when they rummage through the trash. I do this not because I'm hardhearted, but because I live in New York City, and there's really no other choice. Anyone living in any major urban area in America probably does the same.

During recent decades, we have literally dumped severely mentally ill people onto our streets, abandoning them to their disease and delusions. This is a great national shame, hidden in plain view. On July 22 [2003], President Bush's New Freedom Commission on Mental Health released a report that was an opportunity to address this neglect, but it, disgracefully, took a pass.

## The mentally ill are too sick to seek treatment on their own

Most of the mentally ill roaming the streets are too sick to know they are sick. Roughly 50 percent of schizophrenics and those with bipolar disorder do not know they are mentally ill. Therefore, if seeking treatment is left as an entirely voluntary choice—as it has been in recent decades—these people will choose continued illness and misery.

Powerful forces oppose caring for the unwilling mentally ill: the American Civil Liberties Union, which maintains essentially that there is a right to be an untreated schizophrenic; the Scientologists, who hate psychiatry as a matter of faith; and "psychiatric survivors," the formerly mentally ill who were treated involuntarily and are ideologically committed to keeping it from happening to anyone else ever again.

The president's commission aped the language and concerns of this anti-involuntary treatment bloc, calling the mentally ill "consumers" and emphasizing the need for their participation in their "plans for recovery." That's fine, so long as the mentally ill people in question know they are ill.

The focus on "choice" fits with a long-running trend toward deinstitutionalization. In 1955, there were 559,000 people in state psychiatric hospitals. [In 2003] there are less than 50,000. If the situation in 1955 had held, adjusting for population growth, there would be more than 900,000 people in state hospitals today. Many of these people are out in their communities and doing fine, but others are living a nightmare on the streets or in jail.

## Many untreated mentally ill people end up homeless or in jail

There are some 450,000 homeless people in the United States, and about a third are mentally ill. Roughly 16 percent of prisoners in state and local jails have psychiatric illnesses. According to Dr. Fuller Torrey, president of the Treatment Advocacy Center: "The Los Angeles County jail, with 3,400 mentally ill prisoners, is de facto the largest psychiatric inpatient facility in the United States. New York's Rikers Island jail, with 2,800 mentally ill prisoners, is the second-largest."

Opponents of involuntary treatment maintain that the severely mentally ill would choose to get care if only mental health services were better. Nonsense. Says Torrey, "You could set up a suite in the local Hyatt with free coffee and cigarettes and these people would show up, but they still wouldn't take their treatment."

Opponents also argue that the "stigma" of mental illness keeps sick people from admitting that they need help. This is self-defeating nonsense. It is allowing mentally ill people to go untreated and roam the streets, free to do harm to themselves and others, that adds to the stigma of psychiatric disorders.

The severely mentally ill refuse treatment simply as part of their illness. The only answer is to treat them involuntarily, and there is a budding trend toward this solution in state laws. According to Sally Satel and Mary Zdanowicz, critics of the Bush commission's work, "Studies consistently show that the majority of patients initially treated without their consent agree with the decision when asked about it in retrospect."

There is no liberty in psychosis, and it is medication that offers mentally ill people true freedom. Unfortunately, the president's commission lacked the moral courage to make a stark statement to this effect and recommend policies in keeping with it. Meanwhile, on street corners all over America, very sick people are left to rot.

# 14

# Involuntary Treatment Laws Are Dangerous

## Douglas A. Smith

*Douglas A. Smith is an activist who works to end what he perceives as the abuse perpetrated by psychiatry and the laws regulating its practice.*

Many states have enacted outpatient commitment laws whereby people who refuse to comply with an outpatient mental health treatment program can be involuntarily committed to a psychiatric hospital. On the one hand, these new laws change very little because psychiatrists have always had the power to incarcerate people if they allege that a patient has a mental illness and is dangerous. On the other hand, the enactment of such laws perpetuates some dangerous myths. The first of these myths is that mental illnesses are real illnesses with biological causes that can be corrected by psychiatric drugs. In fact, "mental illness" is not a real disease, and psychiatry is only a pseudoscience. Second, these laws support the false idea that psychiatrists are honest experts who make reliable judgments about who is mentally ill and who could become violent. In many cases, psychiatrists lack the integrity and the expertise to make such calls. Finally, outpatient commitment laws may encourage psychiatrists and other mental health "professionals" to hospitalize people only because they refuse to take psychiatric drugs as part of their outpatient program. Psychiatric drugs are harmful and should not be forced on anyone.

Many of us in the ex-patients' or psychiatric survivors' antipsychiatry movement, including myself, have been dismayed by the enactment of "outpatient commitment" laws [which require people to be hospitalized if they refuse to comply with an outpatient treatment program] in most states of the U.S.A. When one version of these laws was enacted in New York ("Kendra's Law"), most of our web sites had initial "blackout" pages to illustrate that the enactment of this law in New York was a black page in the history of the antipsychiatry movement and our campaign for human rights. However, these victories by the supporters of psychiatric op-

Douglas A. Smith, "Why Outpatient Commitment Laws Change (Almost) Nothing," www.antipsychiatry.org, December 19, 1999. Copyright © 1999 by the Antipsychiatry Coalition. Reproduced by permission.

pression in the form of New York's Kendra's Law and similar laws in other states are largely symbolic. In terms of their practical effect, these new laws change almost nothing. My own experience will illustrate why:

Over 30 years ago, I was committed involuntarily by my parents and a psychiatrist they hired who initially insisted my opinion that all human beings have a right to end their lives if they wish was some kind of mental disorder that justified detaining me against my will through involuntary commitment proceedings. My sorrow because of personal problems and having at times thought about ending my life to escape the pain I felt was what motivated my parents to hire the psychiatrist, but I never did decide to end my life nor had I ever made a suicide attempt, and the psychiatrist didn't actually say anything about how sad I felt or that he thought I might decide to end my life in response to my question about why it was appropriate to subject me to an involuntary commitment.

---

*Most psychiatrists I've observed are routinely dishonest.*

---

After about a month of observing me and talking with me on an almost daily basis he told me he'd changed his mind and had decided that while he disagreed with my opinion about everyone having the right to end one's own life, it wasn't really a disorder—and he said he could find no evidence I had a mental illness, just ordinary sorrow that he called "situational, not biological." According to my parents, about the same time he told them I did "not have a serious mental illness."

Two or three weeks later he discharged me from the hospital. However, about two weeks after my release, my mother made an appointment for me to see him because she thought my mood was too serious or sad. The main reason I'd been committed was my refusal to resume so-called outpatient psychotherapy I'd tried months before and found worthless, and after my discharge from the hospital I continued to refuse to be a psychiatric or psychotherapeutic outpatient. I was not being asked to take psychiatric drugs. My parents and their psychiatrist insisted only that I see him at his office for a consultation or what might have been called "psychotherapy." Despite his admission to me and my parents about a month before that I did not have a "mental illness" (at least, not a "serious" one), the psychiatrist, with my parents' support, threatened to commit me again if I refused to see him at his office. I continued to refuse to see him as an outpatient, and for that reason alone—none other—he again committed me against my will to the same hospital, using the "emergency admission" procedure under which I was immediately incarcerated before having any sort of hearing or trial. Of course, to do this, he had to allege that I had a mental illness and was likely to cause injury to myself or others if I was not immediately hospitalized. He knew these allegations were false. They were outright lies. He knew it, and he knew that I knew it. But because it suited his purpose of trying to force me to be an outpatient, he nevertheless made these allegations required by law for an involuntary commitment. *This was many years before anybody was even talking about "outpatient commitment" laws such as Kendra's Law*, under which people may be incarcerated in a hospital only because they refuse to comply with a program of outpatient "treatment."

## Demanding a jury trial

I was able to stop this oppressive use of psychiatric commitment law *only* by demanding a jury trial. I'd learned from my first commitment that failure to demand a jury trial always results in involuntary commitment by a judge who automatically and routinely approves physicians' requests for commitment without even pretending to form his own opinion about the appropriateness of the commitment. For example, the judge who committed me did so without hearing any testimony despite my demand I be permitted to ask the psychiatrist questions (i.e., cross-examine the witnesses against me). The judge said in response that the psychiatrist had submitted his opinion in writing, and despite my protest the judge insisted that was all that was required. My court-appointed attorney (who said literally not one word during my conversation with the judge that passed for a "hearing") ignored my repeated demands he appeal. So the second time I demanded a jury trial. Rather than attempt to persuade a jury he should be permitted to continue to hold me against my will, the psychiatrist released me from the hospital. I've had no psychiatric or psychological "therapy" since then.

## Psychiatrists already have despotic powers

Psychiatrists, and in most states all licensed physicians, have always had the power to incarcerate people involuntarily for any reason they want *if* they are willing to allege "mental illness" and "dangerousness" as required by the state's involuntary commitment law. Since "dangerousness" is a prediction of *future* conduct, it is *always* possible to make this allegation. Since *nobody* can ever prove he or she isn't going to do something in the future, this allegation is always impossible to disprove. In the 30 years I've been observing this I've seen psychiatrists *routinely* make these allegations even when they have no reason to believe they are true and do not really believe the proposed patient is likely to harm anyone. All Kendra's Law and similar "outpatient commitment" laws do is make it unnecessary for the psychiatrist or other physician to tell these lies. Since few psychiatrists are constrained by the bounds of honesty, Kendra's Law and similar outpatient commitment laws do not really expand their despotic powers. The only psychiatrist whose powers are expanded by an outpatient commitment law such as Kendra's Law is one who *always tells the truth*, at least as he or she sees it. I think some psychiatrists are honest—even if most of their "expertise" is nonsense—but most psychiatrists I've observed are routinely dishonest.

So let's see Kendra's Law in New York and similar laws in other states for what they are: *symbolic* victories of those who favor using psychiatry to violate human rights.

## The dangers of the new laws

There are at least two dangers of these new laws:
First, their enactment shows that our lawmakers still believe myths

such as (1) mental illness is a real illness, and it deprives people of free will and of the ability to make rational decisions, (2) mental illnesses are caused by biochemical imbalances that are corrected by psychiatric drugs, and (3) psychiatrists are always honest and are experts in their field, so their "diagnoses" determining who is "mentally ill" and who will become violent are reliable, making safeguards against unnecessary or unjust or oppressive use of involuntary commitment unnecessary. We need to be more effective in our efforts to make lawmakers, judges, mental health professionals, and ourselves realize that physicians are *not* perfect examples of honesty and integrity, that "mental illness" is not a valid concept, that psychiatry is a pseudo-science, that unjust psychiatric commitment is commonplace, that psychiatrists routinely violate human rights, and that psychiatric "treatment" usually harms rather than helps people.

Second, these outpatient commitment laws may get psychiatrists and other mental health "professionals" in the habit of incarcerating people *only* because they refuse to take psychiatric drugs when in the past they might have left us alone. All psychiatric drugs are harmful. *Nobody* should be taking these drugs. If we can't stop the lawful use of coercive psychiatry, we may need to start an "underground railroad" similar to that used to help blacks escape slavery during the period shortly before the civil war when slavery was legal. Does anybody know where victims of psychiatric oppression can go to hide from those who would harm them with involuntary commitment or forced use of psychiatric drugs? Does anybody want to volunteer to provide transportation to such a safe haven?

# 15

# People with Mental Illnesses Should Not Be Imprisoned

## Human Rights Watch

*Human Rights Watch is a nongovernmental organization that investigates and reports on human rights abuses in all regions of the world.*

Mentally ill prisoners are not receiving the treatment they need in U.S. prisons. Although prisoners have rates of mental illness that are two to four times greater than the rates of members of the general public, the prison system has inadequate resources and facilities to care for those who need mental health services. In the worst cases, prisoners have been locked in segregation with no treatment at all or have been abused or ignored by prison staff. Security staff often view the mentally ill as difficult and disorderly and confine them to solitary units. The lack of human interaction and mental health services in these segregation cells only aggravates the suffering of these prisoners and causes further psychiatric breakdown. Many of the growing number of mentally ill people in the prison population are not receiving the treatment they need to be able to reenter society. In order to promote public safety and crime reduction, elected officials need to implement alternatives to incarceration, including drug and mental health treatment programs.

Somewhere between two and three hundred thousand men and women in U.S. prisons suffer from mental disorders, including such serious illnesses as schizophrenia, bipolar disorder, and major depression. An estimated seventy thousand are psychotic on any given day. Yet across the nation, many prison mental health services are woefully deficient, crippled by understaffing, insufficient facilities, and limited programs. All too often seriously ill prisoners receive little or no meaningful treatment. They are neglected, accused of malingering, treated as disciplinary problems.

Without the necessary care, mentally ill prisoners suffer painful symptoms and their conditions can deteriorate. They are afflicted with delusions and hallucinations, debilitating fears, extreme and uncontrollable mood swings. They huddle silently in their cells, mumble incoherently, or yell incessantly. They refuse to obey orders or lash out without apparent provocation. They beat their heads against cell walls, smear themselves with feces, self-mutilate, and commit suicide.

---

*In the United States, there are three times more mentally ill people in prisons than in mental health hospitals.*

---

Prisons were never intended as facilities for the mentally ill, yet that is one of their primary roles today. Many of the men and women who cannot get mental health treatment in the community are swept into the criminal justice system after they commit a crime. In the United States, there are three times more mentally ill people in prisons than in mental health hospitals, and prisoners have rates of mental illness that are two to four times greater than the rates of members of the general public. While there has been extensive documentation of the growing presence of the mentally ill in prison, little has been written about their fate behind bars. . . .

## Mentally ill prisoners are neglected

Our research reveals significant advances in mental health care services in some prison systems. Across the country there are competent and committed mental health professionals who struggle to provide good mental health services to those who need them. They face, however, daunting obstacles—including facilities and rules designed for punishment. The current fiscal crisis in states across the country also threatens the gains that have been made.

Our research also indicates the persistence in many prisons of deep-rooted patterns of neglect, mistreatment, and even cavalier disregard for the well-being of vulnerable and sick human beings. A federal district judge, referring in 1999 to conditions in Texas' prisons, made an observation that is still too widely applicable:

> Whether because of a lack of resources, a misconception of the reality of psychological pain, the inherent callousness of the bureaucracy, or officials' blind faith in their own policies, the [corrections department] has knowingly turned its back on this most needy segment of its population.

In the most extreme cases, conditions are truly horrific: mentally ill prisoners locked in segregation with no treatment at all; confined in filthy and beastly hot cells; left for days covered in feces they have smeared over their bodies; taunted, abused, or ignored by prison staff; given so little water during summer heat waves that they drink from their toilet bowls. A prison expert recently described one prison unit as "medieval . . . cramped, unventilated, unsanitary . . . it will make some men mad and mad men madder." Suicidal prisoners are left naked and unattended for days on end in barren, cold observation cells. Poorly trained correctional officers have accidentally asphyxiated mentally ill prisoners whom they were trying to restrain.

Offenders who need psychiatric interventions for their mental illness should be held in secure facilities if they have committed serious crimes, but those facilities should be designed and operated to meet treatment needs. Society gains little from incarcerating offenders with mental illness in environments that are, at best, counter-therapeutic and, at worst dangerous to their mental and physical well-being. As another federal judge eloquently noted:

> All humans are composed of more than flesh and bone—even those who, because of unlawful and deviant behavior, must be locked away. . . . Mental health, just as much as physical health, is a mainstay of life. Indeed, it is beyond any serious dispute that mental health is a need as essential to a meaningful human existence as other basic physical demands our bodies may make for shelter, warmth, or sanitation.

Doing time in prison is hard for everyone. Prisons are tense and overcrowded facilities in which all prisoners struggle to maintain their self-respect and emotional equilibrium despite violence, exploitation, extortion, and lack of privacy; stark limitations on family and community contacts; and a paucity of opportunities for meaningful education, work, or other productive activities. But doing time in prison is particularly difficult for prisoners with mental illness that impairs their thinking, emotional responses, and ability to cope. They have unique needs for special programs, facilities, and extensive and varied health services. Compared to other prisoners, moreover, prisoners with mental illness also are more likely to be exploited and victimized by other inmates.

## Mental illness keeps prisoners from following the rules

Mental illness impairs prisoners' ability to cope with the extraordinary stresses of prison and to follow the rules of a regimented life predicated on obedience and punishment for infractions. These prisoners are less likely to be able to follow correctional rules. Their misconduct is punished—regardless of whether it results from their mental illness. Even their acts of self-mutilation and suicide attempts are too often seen as "malingering" and punished as rule violations. As a result, mentally ill prisoners can accumulate extensive disciplinary histories.

---

*Society gains little from incarcerating offenders with mental illness in environments that are . . . dangerous to their mental and physical well-being.*

---

Our research suggests that few prisons accommodate their mental health needs. Security staff typically view mentally ill prisoners as difficult and disruptive, and place them in barren high-security solitary confinement units. The lack of human interaction and the limited mental stimulus of twenty-four-hour-a-day life in small, sometimes windowless segregation cells, coupled with the absence of adequate mental health services, dramatically aggravates the suffering of the mentally ill. Some deteriorate so severely that they must be removed to hospitals for acute psychiatric care. But after being stabilized, they are then returned to the same segregation conditions where the cycle of decompensation begins again. The penal network is thus not only serving as a warehouse for the mentally ill, but, by relying on extremely restrictive housing for mentally ill prisoners, it is acting as an *incubator* for worse illness and psychiatric breakdowns.

## U.S. prisons violate international human rights law

International human rights law and standards specifically address conditions of confinement, including the treatment of mentally ill prisoners. If, for example, U.S. officials honored in practice the International Covenant on Civil and Political Rights, to which the United States is a party, and the United Nation's Standard Minimum Rules for the Treatment of Prisoners, which sets out detailed guidelines on how prisoners should be treated, practices in American prisons would improve dramatically. These human rights documents affirm the right of prisoners not to be subjected to cruel, inhuman, or degrading conditions of confinement and the right to mental health treatment consistent with community standards of care. That is, human rights standards do not permit corrections agencies to ignore or undertreat mental illness just because a person is incarcerated. The Eighth Amendment to the U.S. Constitution, which prohibits cruel and unusual punishment, also provides prisoners a right to humane conditions of confinement, including mental health services for serious illnesses.

Prisoners are not, however, a powerful public constituency, and legislative and executive branch officials typically ignore their rights absent litigation or the threat of litigation. U.S. reservations to international human rights treaties mean that prisoners cannot bring suit based on violations of their rights under those treaties. Lawsuits under the U.S. Constitution can only accomplish so much. Federal courts have interpreted the U.S. Constitution as violated only when officials are "deliberately indifferent" to prisoners' known and serious mental health needs. Neglect or malpractice are not constitutional violations. In most states, prisoners cannot sue public officials under state law for medical malpractice. Finally, the misguided Prison Litigation Reform Act, enacted in 1996, has seriously hampered the ability of prisoners to achieve effective and timely help from the courts.

## Mental health services promote safety in the prison community

Mental health treatment can help some people recover from their illness, and for many others it can alleviate its painful symptoms. It can enhance independent functioning and encourage the development of more effective internal controls. In the context of prisons, mental health services play an even broader role. By helping individual prisoners regain health and improve coping skills, they promote safety and order within the prison community as well as offer the prospect of enhancing community safety when the offenders are ultimately released. The components of quality, comprehensive mental health care in prison are well known. They include systematic screening and evaluation for mental illness; mechanisms to provide prisoners with prompt access to mental health personnel and services; mental health treatment that includes a range of appropriate therapeutic interventions including, but not limited to, appropriate medication; a spectrum of levels of care including acute inpatient care and hospitalization, long-term intermediate care programs, and outpatient care; a sufficient number of qualified mental health professionals to develop individualized treatment plans and to implement such plans for all prisoners suffering from serious mental disorders; maintenance of adequate and confidential clinical records and the use of such records to ensure continuity of care as prisoners are transferred from jail to prison and between prisons; suicide prevention protocols for identifying and treating suicidal prisoners; and discharge planning that will provide mentally-ill prisoners with access to needed mental health and other support services upon their release from prison. Peer review and quality assurance programs help ensure that proper policies on paper are translated into practice inside the prisons.

---

*The penal network . . . is acting as an* incubator *for worse illness and psychiatric breakdowns.*

---

Many prison systems have good policies on paper, but implementation can lag far behind. In recent years, some prison systems have begun to implement system-wide reforms—often prompted by litigation—and innovative programs to attend to the mentally ill. Nevertheless, across the country, seriously ill prisoners continue to confront a paucity of qualified staff who can evaluate their illness, develop and implement treatment plans, and monitor their conditions; they confront treatment that consists of little more than medication or no treatment at all; they remain at unnecessarily high risk for suicide and self-mutilation; they live in the chaos of the general prison population or under the strictures of solitary confinement—with brief breaks in a hospital—because of the lack of specialized facilities that would provide the long-term supportive, therapeutically-oriented environment they need.

## Prisons cannot help the mentally ill

Providing mental health services to incarcerated offenders is frustrated by lack of resources. It is also frustrated by the realities of prison life. Correctional mental health professionals work in facilities run by security staff according to rules never designed for or intended to accommodate the mentally ill. For example, mentally ill prisoners are consigned to segregated units even though the harsh, isolated confinement in such units can provoke psychiatric breakdown. Moreover, the rules designed by security staff for prisoners in solitary confinement prevent mental health professionals from providing little more than medication to the mentally ill confined in these units; they cannot provide much needed private counseling, group therapy, and structured activities. Correctional staff who have the most contact with prisoners and who are often called upon to make decisions regarding their needs—particularly in the evenings when mental health staff are not present—often lack the training to recognize symptoms of mental illness and to handle appropriately prisoners who are psychotic or acting in bizarre or even violent ways. It is easy for untrained correctional staff to assume an offender is deliberately breaking the rules or is faking symptoms of illness for secondary gain, such as to obtain a release from solitary confinement into a less harsh hospital setting.

---

*Correctional staff . . . often lack the training to recognize symptoms of mental illness.*

---

Many experts with whom we spoke also noted that, unfortunately, the judgment of some mental health professionals working in prisons becomes compromised over time. They become quick to find malingering instead of illness; to see mentally ill prisoners as troublemakers instead of persons who may be difficult but are nonetheless deserving of serious medical attention. The tendency to limit treatment to the most acutely and patently ill is also encouraged by the lack of resources; since everyone cannot receive appropriate treatment, mental health staff limit their attention to only a few.

## Public policies have created problems

The growing number of mentally ill persons who are incarcerated in the United States is an unintended consequence of two distinct public policies adopted over the last thirty years. First, elected officials have failed to provide adequate funding, support, and direction for the community mental health systems that were supposed to replace the mental health hospitals shut down as part of the "deinstitutionalization" effort that began in the 1960s.

A federal advisory commission appointed by President George W. Bush, the President's New Freedom Commission on Mental Health, recently reported that the U.S. mental health system was "in shambles." People with serious mental illnesses—particularly those who are also poor, homeless, and suffering as well from untreated alcoholism or drug addiction—often cannot obtain the mental health treatment they need. Left untreated and unstable, they enter the criminal justice system when they break the law. Most of their crimes are minor public order or nuisance crimes, but some are felonies which lead to prison sentences.

Second, elected officials have embraced a punitive anti-crime effort, including a national "war on drugs" that dramatically expanded the number of persons brought into the criminal justice system, the number of prison sentences given even for nonviolent crimes (particularly drug and property offenses), and the length of those sentences. Prison and jail populations have soared, more than quadrupling in the last thirty years. A considerable proportion of that soaring prison population consists of the mentally ill.

There is growing recognition in the United States that the country can ill-afford its burgeoning prison population, and that for many crimes, public goals of safety and crime reduction would be equally—if not better—served by alternatives to incarceration, including drug and mental health treatment programs. Momentum is building, albeit slowly, to divert low-level nonviolent offenders from prison—an effort that would benefit many of the mentally ill. But until the country makes radical changes in its approach to community mental health—as well as poverty and homelessness—there is every likelihood that men and women with mental illness will continue to be over-represented among prison populations.

# Organizations to Contact

The editors have compiled the following list of organizations concerned with the issues debated in this book. The descriptions are derived from materials provided by the organizations. All have publications or information available for interested readers. The list was compiled on the date of publication of the present volume; the information provided here may change. Be aware that many organizations take several weeks or longer to respond to inquiries, so allow as much time as possible.

**American Association of Suicidology (AAS)**
4201 Connecticut Ave. NW, Suite 408, Washington, DC 20008
(202) 237-2280 • fax: (202) 237-2282
e-mail: info@suicidology.org • Web site: www.suicidology.org

The association is one of the largest suicide prevention organizations in the nation. It believes that suicidal thoughts are almost always a symptom of depression and that suicide is almost never a rational decision. It publishes the quarterly newsletter *Surviving Suicide*, the journal *Suicide and Life-Threatening Behavior*, and fact sheets.

**American Psychiatric Association (APA)**
1000 Wilson Blvd., Suite 1825, Arlington, VA 22209
(703) 907-7300 • fax: (703) 907-1085
e-mail: apa@psych.org • Web site: www.psych.org

An organization of psychiatrists dedicated to studying the nature, treatment, and prevention of mental disorders, the APA helps create mental health policies, distributes information about psychiatry, and promotes psychiatric research and education. It publishes the *American Journal of Psychiatry* monthly and a variety of books and newsletters.

**American Psychological Association (APA)**
750 First St. NE, Washington, DC 20002-4242
(202) 336-5500 • fax: (202) 336-5708
e-mail: public.affairs@apa.org • Web site: www.apa.org

The American Psychological Association is the largest scientific and professional organization representing psychology in the United States and is the world's largest association of psychologists. It publishes numerous books, journals, and videos.

**Canadian Mental Health Association (CMHA)**
8 King St. East, Suite 810, Toronto, ON M5C 1B5 Canada
(416) 484-7750 • fax: (416) 484-4617
e-mail: national@cmha.ca • Web site: www.cmha.ca

The Canadian Mental Health Association is one of the oldest voluntary organizations in Canada. Its programs are designed to assist people suffering from mental illness find the help needed to cope with crises, regain confidence, and return to their communities, families, and jobs. It publishes books, reports, policy statements, and pamphlets.

## Children and Adults with Attention-Deficit/Hyperactivity Disorder (CHADD)
8181 Professional Pl., Suite 150, Landover, MD 20785
(800) 233-4050 • (301) 306-7070 • fax: (301) 306-7090
e-mail: national@chadd.org • Web site: www.chadd.org

CHADD is a nonprofit organization founded by a group of concerned parents that works to improve the lives of children and adults with attention-deficit/ hyperactivity disorder through education, advocacy, and support. It publishes the quarterly *Attention!* magazine, books, and many fact sheets about the disorder.

## Citizens Commission on Human Rights (CCHR)
6616 Sunset Blvd., Los Angeles, CA 90028
(800) 869-2247 • (323) 467-4242 • fax: (323) 467-3720
e-mail: humanrights@cchr.org • Web site: www.cchr.org

CCHR is a nonprofit organization whose goal is to expose and eradicate criminal acts and human rights abuses by psychiatry. The organization believes that psychiatric drugs cause insanity and violence. CCHR publishes numerous books, including *Psychiatry: Destroying Morals* and *Psychiatry: Education's Ruin*.

## False Memory Syndrome Foundation
1955 Locust St., Philadelphia, PA 19103
(215) 940-1040 • fax: (215) 940-1042
e-mail: mail@fmsonline.org • Web site: www.fmsonline.org

The foundation was established to combat False Memory Syndrome (FMS), a condition in which patients are led by their therapists to "remember" traumatic incidents—usually childhood sexual abuses—that never actually occurred. The foundation seeks to assist the victims of FMS and people falsely accused of committing child sexual abuse through publicity, counseling, and research. It publishes the *FMS Foundation Newsletter* and distributes information and articles on FMS.

## International Society for the Study of Dissociation (ISSD)
60 Ravere Dr., Suite 500, Northbrook, IL 60062
(847) 480-0899 • fax: (847) 480-9282
e-mail: info@issd.org • Web site: www.issd.org

The society's membership comprises mental health professionals and students interested in dissociation. It conducts research and promotes improved understanding of this condition. It publishes the quarterly journal *Dissociation* and a quarterly newsletter.

## National Alliance for Research on Schizophrenia and Depression (NARSAD)
60 Cutter Mill Rd., Suite 404, Great Neck, NY 11021
(800) 829-8289 • (516) 829-0091 • fax: (516) 487-6930
e-mail: info@narsad.org • Web site: www.narsad.org

The alliance is a nonprofit coalition of citizens' groups that raises funds for research into the causes, treatments, cures, and prevention of severe mental illnesses. It publishes *NARSAD Research*, a quarterly newsletter.

**National Alliance for the Mentally Ill (NAMI)**
Colonial Place Three, 2107 Wilson Blvd., Suite 300, Arlington, VA 22201
(703) 524-7600 • fax: (703) 524-9094
Web site: www.nami.org

NAMI is a consumer advocacy and support organization composed largely of family members of people with severe mental illnesses such as schizophrenia, manic-depressive illness, and depression. The alliance adheres to the position that severe mental illnesses are biological brain diseases and that mentally ill people should not be blamed or stigmatized for their condition. Its publications include the bimonthly newsletter *NAMI Advocate* and the book *Breakthroughs in Antipsychotic Medications.*

**National Association for Rural Mental Health (NARMH)**
3700 W. Division St., Suite 105, St. Cloud, MN 56301
(320) 202-1820 • fax: (320) 202-1833
e-mail: narmh@facts.ksu.edu • Web site: www.narmh.org

The association consists of mental health professionals, administrators, and other people dedicated to improving mental health services in rural areas. It provides training to mental health practitioners, and it promotes the use of mental health services by those living in rural communities. NARMH publishes the quarterly *Rural Community Health Newsletter* and distributes occasional position statements.

**National Association of Psychiatric Health Systems (NAPHS)**
325 Seventh St., Suite 625, Washington, DC 20004-1154
(202) 393-6700 • fax: (202) 783-6041
e-mail: naphs@naphs.org • Web site: www.naphs.org

The association represents the interests of private psychiatric hospitals, residential treatment centers, and programs partially consisting of hospital care. It provides a forum for ideas concerning the administration, care, and treatment of the mentally ill. It publishes various fact sheets, policy recommendations, and advocate information, including *How You Can Help Reform Mental Health: A Grassroots Guide to Political Action.*

**National Foundation for Depressive Illness (NAFDI)**
PO Box 2257, New York, NY 10116
(800) 239-1265
Web site: www.depression.org

NAFDI provides information about depression and manic-depressive illness. It promotes the view that these disorders are physical illnesses treatable with medication, and it believes that such medication should be made readily available to those who need it. The foundation publishes the quarterly newsletter *NAFDI News* and the fact sheet "Symptoms of Depression and Manic Depression."

**National Institute of Mental Health (NIMH)**
6001 Executive Blvd., Room 8184, MSC 9663, Bethesda, MD 20892-9663
(301) 443-4513 • fax: (301) 443-4279
e-mail: nimhinfo@nih.gov • Web site: www.nimh.nih.gov

NIMH is the federal agency concerned with mental health research. It plans and conducts a comprehensive program of research relating to the causes, prevention, diagnosis, and treatment of mental illnesses. It produces various informational publications on mental disorders and their treatment.

**National Mental Health Association (NMHA)**
2001 N. Beauregard St., Twelfth Floor, Alexandria, VA 22311
(800) 433-5959 • fax: (703) 684-5968
e-mail: nmhainfo@aol.com • Web site: www.nmha.org

The association is a consumer advocacy organization concerned with combating mental illness and improving mental health. It promotes research into the treatment and prevention of mental illness, monitors the quality of care provided to the mentally ill, and provides educational materials on mental illness and mental health. It publishes the monthly newsletter *The Bell* as well as books and pamphlets on understanding and overcoming mental illness.

**Obsessive-Compulsive Foundation (OCF)**
676 State St., New Haven, CT 06511
(203) 401-2070 • fax: (203) 401-2076
e-mail: info@ocfoundation.org • Web site: www.ocfoundation.org

The foundation consists of individuals with obsessive-compulsive disorders (OCDs), their friends and families, and the professionals who treat them. It works to increase public awareness of and discover a cure for obsessive-compulsive disorders. It publishes the bimonthly *OCD Newsletter* and the pamphlet *OCD Questions and Answers*.

**Suicide Awareness Voices of Education (SAVE)**
7317 Cahill Rd., Suite 207, Minneapolis, MN 55439-2080
(952) 946-7998
e-mail: save@save.org • Web site: www.save.org

The mission of SAVE is to educate about suicide prevention and to speak for suicide survivors. It publishes the reports "What to Do If Someone You Know Becomes Suicidal" and "Q & A on Depression."

# Bibliography

## Books

Nancy C. Andreason — *Brave New Brain: Conquering Mental Illness in the Era of the Genome.* New York: Oxford University Press, 2001.

Alex Beam — *Gracefully Insane: Life and Death Inside America's Premier Mental Hospital.* New York: PublicAffairs, 2003.

Karen Bellenir, ed. — *Mental Health Disorders Sourcebook: Basic Consumer Health Information About Anxiety Disorders, Depression, and Other Mood Disorders.* Detroit, MI: Omnigraphics, 2000.

Floyd E. Bloom, M. Flint Beal, and David J. Jupfer, eds. — *The Dana Guide to Brain Health.* New York: Free Press, 2003.

Peter R. Breggin — *The Anti-Depressant Fact Book: What Your Doctor Won't Tell You About Prozac, Zoloft, Paxil, Celexa, and Luvox.* Cambridge, MA: Perseus, 2001.

Max Fink — *Electroshock: Restoring the Mind.* New York: Oxford University Press, 1999.

William Glasser — *Warning: Psychiatry Can Be Hazardous to Your Mental Health.* New York: HarperCollins, 2003.

Joseph Glenmullen — *Prozac Backlash.* New York: Simon and Schuster, 2000.

David Healy — *The Creation of Psychopharmacology.* Cambridge, MA: Harvard University Press, 2002.

J. Allan Hobson and Jonathon A. Leonard — *Out of Its Mind: Psychiatry in Crisis.* Cambridge, MA: Perseus, 2001.

James Johnson and John D. Preston — *Clinical Psychopharmacology Made Ridiculously Simple.* Miami, FL: Medmaster, 2001.

Richard A. Moskovitz — *Lost in the Mirror: An Inside Look at Borderline Personality Disorder.* Dallas, TX: Taylor, 2001.

Peter E. Nathan and Jack M. Gorman — *A Guide to Treatments That Work.* New York: Oxford University Press, 2002.

Richard O'Connor — *Active Treatment of Depression.* New York: W.W. Norton, 2001.

Elyn R. Saks — *Refusing Care: Forced Treatment and the Rights of the Mentally Ill.* Chicago: University of Chicago Press, 2002.

Stephen B. Seager — *Street Crazy: America's Mental Health Tragedy.* Redondo Beach, CA: Westcom, 2000.

E. Fuller Torrey and Michael B. Knable — *Surviving Manic Depression: A Manual on Bipolar Disorder for Patients, Families, and Providers.* New York: Basic Books, 2002.

Elliot Valenstein — *Blaming the Brain: The Truth About Drugs and Mental Health.* New York: Free Press, 2002.

Robert Whitaker — *Mad in America: Bad Science, Bad Medicine, and the Enduring Mistreatment of the Mentally Ill.* Cambridge, MA: Perseus, 2002.

## Periodicals

Stacey Burling — "Implant Could Help Schizophrenics Stay Medicated, Raises Ethical Concerns," *Philadelphia Inquirer*, September 30, 2003.

Elizabeth Daigneau — "Criminal Hospital," *Congressional Quarterly*, September 2002.

David Davis — "Losing the Mind," *Los Angeles Times Magazine*, October 26, 2003.

John Gibeaut — "Who Knows Best?" *ABA Journal*, January 2000.

Richard M. Glass — "Electroconvulsive Therapy: Time to Bring It Out of the Shadows," *JAMA*, 2001.

Frederic Golden — "The Hunt for Cures: Mental Illness Probing the Chemistry of the Brain," *Time*, January 15, 2001.

Katherine Hodges — "The Invisible Crisis: Women and Psychiatric Oppression," *Off Our Backs*, July/August 2003.

Carla McClain — "Drugs, Talk Best for Depression," *Tucson Citizen*, June 6, 2000.

Paul Murphy and Annie Murphy — "Self-Help: Shattering the Myths," *Psychology Today*, March/April 2001.

Kelly Patricia O'Meara — "Baughman Dispels the Myth of ADHD," *Insight Magazine*, February 18, 2002.

Michael A. Pawel — "Imprisoning the Mentally Ill: Does It Matter?" *Criminal Justice Ethics*, January 1, 2001.

Kaja Perina — "Battling for Benefits: When HMOs Curb Mental-Health Care, the Consequences Can Be Lethal," *Psychology Today*, March/April 2002.

Robert Sapolsky — "Taming Stress: An Emerging Understanding of the Brain's Stress Pathways Points Toward Treatments for Anxiety and Depression Beyond Valium and Prozac," *Scientific American*, September 2003.

Daniel Smith — "Shock and Disbelief," *Atlantic Monthly*, February 2001.

Carla Spartos — "Sarafem Nation," *Village Voice*, December 12, 2000.

Marcello Spinella — "Psychoactive Herbal Medications," *Skeptical Inquirer*, January 2001.

Marianne
Szegedy-Maszak
"The Demons of Childhood," *U.S. News & World Report,*
November 11, 2002.

E. Fuller Torrey
"Hippie Healthcare Policy: While One Government Agency Searches for the Cure to Mental Diseases, Another Clings to the '60s Notion That They Don't Exist," *Washington Monthly*, April 2002.

Shankar Vedantam
"Rush to Medicate Mental Illness Raises Concerns," *Philadelphia Inquirer*, March 24, 2001.

L. Jon Wertheim
"Prisoners of Depression," *Sports Illustrated*, September 8, 2003.

# Index